PIKE

PIKE

Dave Phillips

Beekay Publishers

Other angling titles by Beekay Publishers:

Coarse

Carp Fever by Kevin Maddocks
The Art of Pole Fishing by Dickie Carr
Pike Fishing in the 80's by Neville Fickling
Basic Carp Fishing by Peter Mohan
Modern Specimen Hunting by Jim Gibbinson
Top Ten—tactics for the major species from ten leading anglers
Edited by Bruce Vaughan
Redmire Pool by Kevin Clifford & Len Arbery
Tactics for Big Pike by Bill Chillingworth
In Pursuit of Carp & Catfish by Kevin Maddocks
Cypry The Carp by Peter Mohan
The Beekay Guide to 450 Carp Waters
Jim Davidson Gets Hooked by Jim Davidson
In Pursuit of Predatory Fish by Neville Fickling
Tiger Bay by Rob Maylin
Understanding Barbel by Fred Crouch
Big-Water Carp by Jim Gibbinson
Mega-Pike by Eddie Turner

Sea

Boat Fishing at Sea by Phill Williams & Brian Douglas
Long Range Casting & Fishing Techniques by Paul Kerry
Cod Fishing by John Rawle
Uptide & Boatcasting by Bob Cox

Game

The Colour Guide to Fly Tying by Kevin Hyatt
Robson's Guide to Stillwater Trout Flies by Kenneth Robson
Dressed to Kill by Bob Carnill & Kenneth Robson

First published in 1990 by
BEEKAY PUBLISHERS
WITHY POOL, BEDFORD ROAD,
HENLOW CAMP, BEDS. SG16 6EA
© Beekay Publishers 1990
ISBN 0 947674 32 2

Typeset by BP Integraphics Ltd., Bath, Avon
Printed in Great Britain at The Bath Press, Avon

About the Author

Dave Phillips was born and bred in the fenlands of west Norfolk, where he caught his first 20 lb-plus pike shortly after his 15th birthday. He has gone on to take many more big pike from all over the British Isles.

During a five-year spell as editor of *Coarse Fisherman*, Dave adopted a campaigning stance and instigated the moves to get Llandegfedd Reservoir opened up to pike angling. It has since produced a record pike as well as several others over 40 lb.

Other notable successes scored included the action taken to prevent an upsurge of boating on the fen drains and the battle to protect the aquatic environment of Norfolk's Broadland ... an area which has since been designated a National Park.

Dave was among the new generation of dedicated pike anglers who, during the early 1980s, helped transform the sport into the popular pursuit it has become today. Working with fellow enthusiasts like Eddie Turner and Neville Fickling, Dave helped develop the sunken float rig and publicised the deadly smelt deadbait ... methods which are invaluable to today's pike anglers.

Now 34, Dave lives in rural Warwickshire and works as a senior journalist on a daily newspaper. He is still actively involved in pike fishing and is currently making great strides in applying American lure-fishing techniques to pike fishing in this country.

Dedication

To my wife, Ilse

Contents

Front Cover: Perch pattern Rapala accounted for this specimen.

Drawings by Len Gurd.

Acknowledgements

Thanks first to my father, who way back in 1966 encouraged me to go fishing in the first place. Thanks also to the great pike anglers of the sixties, whose written exploits inspired kids like Neville Fickling and myself to attempt to emulate them.

Neville, of course, went on to better their achievements—as did my great mate Eddie Turner. My own enjoyment and catches would have been much poorer without the influence and company of those two extreme characters!

Pike angling is full of harmless eccentrics, most of whom I seem to have either fished with, drank with or swapped yarns with. I owe you all a debt of gratitude.

A special thank-you to Neville, Eddie and Graham Billing for the loan of photographs used in this book and, last but not least, thanks to my understanding wife Ilse for tolerating the whims and unsociable hours of a lifelong pike angler.

Dave Phillips, April 1990.

Introduction

The pike is without doubt Britain's most talked-about fish. It's big, power-ful and—to the uninformed—an ugly, greedy predator. Virtually every angler has a tale to tell about the pike's supposedly prodigious appetite ... and even non-angling members of the public often have a piece of outrageous pike lore to relate.

As a result, somewhere back in angling history, the pike earned the tag 'freshwater shark'. Of course, it is in no way related to the shark family, but its somewhat fearsome appearance was undoubtedly respon-sible for that misnomer. Nature gave the pike a long, streamlined body, a pointed snout and an awesome set of very sharp teeth. The unusual (for a coarse fish) position of its eyes gives it the advantage of binocular vision—and caused countless angling writers through the ages to remark upon its so-called 'baleful glare'.

Fear of the unknown has always caused Man's imagination to run riot. In the case of the pike, this has spawned a rich vein of legend. Fred Buller has documented many of these fables in his *Domesday Book of Mammoth Pike*—and very entertaining they are too. But the object of this book is not to perpetrate myth, but to enable the reader to catch more and better pike through understanding the facts about his chosen species.

Contrary to folklore, pike do not attack the limbs of unsuspecting bathers. Nor do they attempt to make a meal from the snouts of cattle drinking at the waterside. In fact even the oft-described ambushes of waterfowl are comparatively rare. Only once in 24 years of angling have I witnessed a pike take a bird— in this case a moorhen— from the surface of the water.

And, sadly, pike do not attain a length of six feet or more. I only wish they did!

So let's forget the exaggerations and get down to the facts. The pike—*Esox lucius*—is the most successful freshwater predatory fish in the north-

Well spotted: A beautifully-marked 12 lb pike from a Peterborough gravel pit. Most reasonable venues in this country are capable of producing pike of this size.

ern hemisphere. Those same physical features which, over the ages, filled Man with such dread, have also contributed to its position at the head of the food chain on countless lakes and rivers in Europe and North America. Its adaptability to a wide range of environments have made it very widespread and an ideal target for the angler.

On most waters in the British Isles you can expect to catch pike averaging 3–7 lb, and even a very mediocre pike fishery will generally turn up occasional double-figure specimens of 10 lb or more. By the time a female pike has reached this weight it is likely to measure 32–35 inches long. Male pike, for some reason, seldom exceed 7–8 lb in weight.

The ultimate size of the pike to be expected at your chosen venue depends upon the fertility of the water and angling pressure. A good, clean environment with healthy stocks of other species of coarse fish of all sizes will, all things being equal, produce excellent pike.

In most areas, and on the majority of waters, a pike of 10 lb or more is considered a good fish. I'll certainly never tire of catching pike of that calibre, even though most venues are also capable of producing pike of 20 lb or more.

Pike of 20 lb-plus are, however, quite rare on all but the richest waters and can be considered real specimens in any angler's book. Only an exceptional individual is likely to grow to the 20 lb mark. At this stage the pike is usually at least six years old, more likely eight, and possibly as old as 14 years. Most pike topping 20 lb are around 40 inches long, although some very rich waters can produce very plump specimens as short as 35 inches which make the grade.

Exceptional pike fisheries will turn up pike of 25 lb or more from time to time, while just a handful are capable of yielding the real monsters; 30 lb-plus mega-pike that few anglers are privileged to witness, let alone catch.

Reading the angling press, it is sometimes easy for the newcomers to big-fish angling to get the impression that 30 lb pike are being caught all over the place. Those same novices will, on occasion, rush out with their newly-acquired pike tackle and expect to start hooking 30-pounders straight away. They are doomed to disappointment.

It is important to get things into perspective. When a pike of 30 lb hits the headlines in the weekly angling papers, you must bear in mind that that fish was the best the country's 3 million anglers could manage between them that week. At the time of writing I'm still eagerly anticipating my own debut 'thirty' . . . but I'm enjoying the satisfaction of coming close from time to time.

My own love affair with the pike was, perhaps, inevitable. Our paths crossed on my very first fishing trip, back in September 1966, on the banks of a tiny Fenland drain close to my parents' West Norfolk home. Accompanied by my father and armed with a home-made solid bamboo rod, centre-pin reel and 6 lb line, I went out prepared to do battle with whatever felt suicidal enough to take on my whole lobworm bait and submerge a very large 'bobber' float.

Like most ten-year-olds, my attention soon wandered from the job in hand. Within an hour, I had left Dad in charge of my gear while I puddled around at the water's edge a few yards away. It was then that a very obliging perch chose to hang itself and was duly landed, unhooked and released by my father.

That episode (which, incidentally, I still vividly recall) was enough to rekindle my enthusiasm and I was soon in charge of the tackle again, awaiting my first bite.

The following sequence of events flashed by very quickly, but I can still picture that bulbous float plunging under at speed, followed by a

Heavyweight: Rich, productive waters will turn up pike like this 27 lb-plus drain fish.

Predator: The beautiful lines of a big pike.

brief flurry of resistance before I reeled in a limp and hook-less line.

My father told me a perch had probably taken my worm bait and had, in turn, been grabbed by a pike, which had subsequently bitten through the line. But in retrospect I'm confident a pike had itself taken a fancy to my wavering tangle of lobworm. Pike are enthusiastic feeders on food other than the fish diet we all know so much about.

That eventful debut outing turned out to be the first in a long series of blanks on my part! But besides that fleeting encounter with an unseen pike in my own swim, I also witnessed the capture of a lovely 12-pounder by another angler a couple of hundred yards along the bank. Not a bad initiation, I guess.

Perhaps I should have marked that swim down as a possible pike hotspot—for that's just what it turned out to be. Less than five years later it produced my first-ever pike of 20 lb-plus, as well as numbers of other nice fish.

During my early fishing years it was very useful to have such a prolific free fishery on my doorstep. The drain in question was a mere two-mile cycle ride from home and an ideal venue on which to learn about pike. It's an apprenticeship I wouldn't have missed for the world and it stood me in good stead for future ventures onto more challenging venues further afield.

Later in this book we will look at the location of pike in various types of venues, as well as the tackle, techniques and baits required to catch them. But in the meantime I would advise any youngster or relative newcomer to start his piking career on a good water within easy travelling distance of his home base.

Don't start flitting from venue to venue according to where the latest newsworthy catches have been made. Fishing for pike which have already received a hammering from other anglers is an exercise in futility. It's the men who find the pike first who make the big catches.

No! Make regular trips to your own water and get to understand its moods in all conditions. Attack the pike with every technique at your disposal and note their preferences; you'll learn much more about the pike and its habits by adopting a thoughtful approach. Only when you are confident you have got to grips with your chosen venue is it time to think about moving on to other waters.

Of course, one of the biggest fascinations of piking has to be its sheer variety. With pike found in virtually every freshwater fishery in this country, there is plenty of scope for the pike angler. And while a river or lake has to be rather special to produce, say, specimen 2 lb roach or 8 lb bream, what we would consider very ordinary coarse fisheries frequently turn out to be excellent pike waters.

Rather poor waters which are hard-pressed to produce roach over 12 oz and bream more than 3 lb are often very good bets for quality pike fishing. So long as the water contains plenty of 'fodder' fish in the 2–12 oz range, it has the potential to produce pike over 20 lb.

... Unless, of course, you are unfortunate enough to live in one of those isolated areas of the country where pike are still regarded as 'vermin' and subject to ignorant abuse from local anglers. From Wales to Wessex, South Yorkshire to Scotland, there are still pockets of anti-pike prejudice—which is almost always down to ignorance. There are still anglers around willing to believe the pike is a voracious wrecker of fisheries, instead of accepting the species as the invaluable pinnacle of our freshwater food chain.

Many fine specimen pike are destroyed by the pike killers every autumn and winter. It's a shocking waste of valuable specimen fish, for

Early days: 1973 and the writer (right) and teenage angling partner Andrew Mack
pose with a bag of pike to 15 lb from a tiny Fen drain.

many of these pike would be fish of a lifetime to some anglers. Happily, the practice of wanton pike killing is on the wane. The process of education, along with today's breed of conservation-minded anglers, is seeing pike killing becoming a thing of the past.

The biggest danger to pike stocks today in fact comes from keen pike anglers who would not dream of deliberately killing a pike, but in fact do enormous harm through ignorance of hooking and handling techniques. Later we'll go into the specialised methods that modern pikers use to ensure no harm comes to their quarry. The massive boom in popularity of pike fishing has put pike stocks under a great deal of angling pressure, so it is imperative that we all do our utmost to preserve future sport.

In writing this book, I have set myself the task of offering detailed information on pike angling which will prove invaluable to novices to our branch of the sport, yet at the same time provide food for thought for the experienced pike men. In order to accomplish this, I am assuming the reader is not a complete beginner to angling, but has already fished for a year or more for other species and has received a basic grounding in general angling techniques. In short, he is primed and ready to take on the challenge of piking.

As so often happens, newcomers to coarse fishing spend a period of time trying all forms of fishing before deciding to specialise in one particular branch of the sport. Some turn to match fishing, others to specimen hunting, and many continue as out-and-out pleasure anglers, more than happy to accept whatever comes along and sucks their maggots.

But whatever direction their angling career eventually takes them, most at some stage will flirt briefly with piking. Whether the angler has inclinations towards specimen hunting and fancies attempting to connect himself with a 20 lb-plus lunker, or just to pull in a bag of medium-sized pike, this book truly describes a species which caters for all tastes.

Even the angler with competitive inclinations can avoid the gruelling winter league matches, if he feels so inclined, to participate in the proliferation of pike matches which are staged these days. Many hard-line pike anglers hold strong views against pike matches, but it is a fact that they are here to stay. Personally I do not participate in pike matches these days, as my own requirements from pike fishing are of a very personal nature. But very many anglers *do* support these competitions, as evidenced by the popularity of the ACA/Angling Times event, where tickets are always at a real premium.

In fact pike matches are unlike any other form of competitive angling in that specimen pike do have a habit of turning up at not infrequent intervals. Indeed, many of these matches have been won by the chap who landed, say, a solitary pike of 20 lb-plus or two or three double-figure specimens.

Luck does indeed play a major part in pike fishing, just as it does to a greater or lesser degree in all forms of angling. A big pike can be as perverse and unobliging as the next fish and refuse all offerings, yet a few hours later might accept the simple sprat bait offered by a complete beginner on his very first cast. But that does not mean fate and fortune are the determining factors dictating success in piking. Most of us get lucky breaks from time to time, but to prove yourself as a successful pike angler you have to achieve consistent results.

To attain success in this branch of the sport you must be prepared to be single-minded. You won't succeed with the pike on a regular basis if you don't take on the task of catching them in a wholehearted fashion. It's no use throwing in a pike bait to look after itself while you are roach fishing, for you must concentrate on the job in hand. Piking as an afterthought is a particularly ineffective way of catching pike ... and what's more the unattended pike rod can result in deeply-hooked and damaged pike stocks.

To the outsider, pike fishing might, on occasions, appear to be a slow old game. The lone piker you see on the far bank of the gravel pit probably looks pretty inactive to you, but if he is a successful pike angler he is putting a lot of thought into his fishing.

The competent piker is actively visualising what his livebait is doing beneath the surface and he just *knows* that he has cast his deadbait to exactly the right spot ... possibly onto the slope of a gravel bar 80 yards out into what the outsider believes is a featureless stillwater.

That same pike angler may have spent the close season walking a length of river, wearing Polaroids and making careful mental notes of potential pike lies. Many keen pike anglers wouldn't even dream of tackling a stillwater unless they had first spent hours with a boat and echo-sounder, mapping out all the depth contours and other pikey features. Others still will read the match reports in the weekly angling press and watch the pleasure anglers—noting just what swims the fodder fish are coming from. Such attention to detail goes a long way to achieving the successful consistent results we are looking for.

We'll look at all these things later in this book, as we examine the potential of pike waters up and down the country. I'll take you with me to the lonely, wind-swept drains of Fenland and on to the incomparable

Feeding frenzy: The writer with a big pike that made a meal of a 3 lb pike whilst it was being played! The teethmarks on the smaller pike can be clearly seen near the dorsal fin.

reedy wastes of the Norfolk Broads. We'll visit the big gravel pits ... the small pools ... the mighty Irish loughs and Scottish lochs and the daunting concrete bowls of some English reservoirs.

Location, coupled with the tackle, techniques and baits you'll require, will put you well on the road to becoming a successful pike angler. I won't be describing complicated and cluttered rigs, because most of them were designed in the first instance by armchair pike anglers trying to solve non-existent problems. Instead, I'll give you the low-down on tried-and-tested methods which have produced a lot of big pike for my friends and myself.

Over the years I've become acutely aware of the constant thirst for knowledge from enthusiastic anglers. I sincerely hope that the following chapters go some way towards quenching that thirst.

As a young and inexperienced pike angler back in the halcyon days I mentioned earlier in this chapter, I was inspired by the writings and exploits of anglers like Fred Wagstaffe, Barrie Rickards and Frank Wright—great pike men all. If this book goes some way towards helping a new generation of pike anglers share the great sport I've enjoyed these past 20-odd years, then the task of writing it will have proved most worth-while.

Please remember — litter loses fishing

Location

Location is the single most important factor determining success or failure in pike fishing—yet among the majority of pike anglers it is often entirely neglected. You can own the best tackle in the world and secure a super supply of dead and livebaits, yet they alone will never catch you pike that simply aren't there. Take pot luck on location and your catches will suffer every time.

The very best bags of pike are made by competent anglers in the right place at the right time. It is also quite possible, with a little thought, to extract a pleasing catch of pike by fishing in the right place at the *wrong* time. Nobody, however, can be successful in the wrong swim at *any* time!

The first step in pike location is selecting the water you intend to fish. If you live in the southern counties, it's odds-on a gravel pit will be your starting point, while midlands anglers will most likely choose reservoirs and East Anglian pikers will turn to drains and broads. As I've already suggested, it is a distinct advantage to pick a venue within reasonable travelling distance of your home in order to put as much time in as possible.

Not everybody is fortunate enough to enjoy top-class pike fishing right on their doorstep, but those who are can fish short, opportunist sessions at the drop of a hat. It is surprising how productive a snatched two-hour trip can be—particularly if you know your water well and have identified the feeding patterns of its pike. If, for example, you get most runs on your water at the crack of dawn, then it doesn't take a genius to recognise the value of a few snatched trips before work . . .

Good pike waters aren't difficult to find. Most areas of the country can boast a few and it's up to you to find them. You can follow up the advice of local anglers and tackle dealers by concentrating on the venues they will tell you have a pikey reputation . . . and it's likely you'll catch some pike. In many areas, however, you'll end up crowded in by

Double delight: Dave with a 17 lb-plus pike from a small Fen drain.

other pikers who have tapped in to the same angling grapevine.

It's all a matter of taste, of course. The more gregarious among us might actually prefer to partake of our piking among hordes of fellow pikers. I like good company when I'm fishing, too, but I must admit I enjoy a quieter scenario for most of the time. Besides, there is a lot more satisfaction in discovering your own pike water and reaping the benefits before word gets out and the hordes descend.

So what sort of venues are we looking for? Although my own piking career started on the drains of Fenland, I'd hazard a guess that the majority of pikers will be looking to their local pits or lakes for most of their sport. And for the beginner to piking, I'd say this would be a wise choice—for a start you won't have floods and raging torrents to contend with and physical underwater features will tend to remain constant (on rivers they are ever-changing).

My own favourite type of stillwater is large, with plenty of features. I've taken big pike from small pits in the past, but I can see little pleasure in catching the same individual pike over and over again—which *will* inevitably happen on any water smaller than about 10 acres. Sure, repeat captures are unavoidable on any pike fisheries—on several occasions I have caught the same pike twice in the space of half an hour in the same swim— but fishing on very small stillwaters is a sure way of becoming close friends with a small number of pike.

I like plenty of features because they make location of pike so much easier. Many gravel pits have bars, points, channels, extensive shallows, weedbeds and snaggy areas—all of which make finding the pike simpler.

Back in 1971, Barrie Rickards and Ray Webb came up with what, at the time, was a revolutionary concept in pike location. In their book, *Fishing For Big Pike,* they suggested that pike were not scattered about the water like so many currants in a cake, but tended to congregate in large numbers in relatively small, but defined areas. Such places they termed hotspots.

That new thinking was eagerly embraced by the keen anglers of the time, who found that it fitted neatly with their own experiences on many waters. Indeed, pike fishing never looked back.

To catch big pike, it was necessary to first find the hotspots. But some unscrupulous pike anglers took a short cut by following successful pike anglers around to discover where they were fishing. In fact Barrie Rickards himself on several occasions found such undesirables firmly ensconced in his best swims, perhaps giving him cause to rue the decision to publish his hotspot findings!

However, natural justice prevailed when it was discovered that undue piking pressure quickly dispersed the pike in the new-found hotspots. In fact sport soon became luke-warm or even stone-cold once the specimen hunters moved into the hotspots to give them a hammering.

Of course, the same still holds true today. On many of our more popular fisheries the pike populations are literally hammered day-in and day-out, with venues like Abberton Reservoir in Essex playing host to a permanent population of pike hunters every day of the autumn and winter on the popular culvert swims. In view of the pasting that water's pike have received from a relatively short bank space over the past decade or more, it is a surprise that the pike are ever foolish enough to feed in that area. It is the common consensus of opinion among the regulars at Abberton that staggering catches of big pike could be made if only angling were allowed on other sections of the reservoir—notably the out-of-bounds valve tower.

Suffice it to say that pike do wise up in the face of heavy angling pressure, although possibly not to the same degree as certain other species—notably the carp. I also believe that pike do associate certain areas

Hotspot pike: These two big fish came on the feed simultaneously.

with danger (i.e. previous captures), but will frequently succumb to the temptation of heavy stocks of food even in danger areas. The problem for the angler on such occasions is likely to be dropped runs and takes that are very difficult to hit. I don't want to give the impression that the pike is a particularly intelligent creature—it certainly is not—but its survival instincts are well up to recognising capture as an unpleasant and injurious hazard.

Early in 1983, acting on a tip given to me by Bob Church, I paid a visit to a short stretch of a small Lincolnshire drain where one of Bob's trout-fishing pals had seen some signs of pike activity. On that very first visit I was fortunate enough to land slap-bang-wallop on a true hotspot, as defined by Rickards and Webb, and landed a very big haul of pike, including seven double-figure specimens to 18 lb. The same tiny area of water also produced five runs which I missed and another five were dropped like the proverbial hot potato.

Obviously one can put up with the frustrations of dropped and missed runs when a big haul of pike is on the cards, so two days later I returned to the swim with a mate. But on the second occasion the pike were even more finicky—and out of 25 runs we managed to hit and land just two very lightly-hooked pike!

Unbeknown to me, other pike anglers had also been fishing quite hard on this same small drain and the pike had seen enough of dry land to become cautious in the extreme. In fact among those fishing it was Keith Mottram of Sheffield, a very successful pike angler, who seldom fished anywhere else at that time! No wonder those pike were spooky.

So although Rickards and Webb's hotspot theory still stands up, you have to bear in mind that it normally applies only to lightly-fished waters. On the typical gravel pit we are talking about, it is a better bet for the pike angler to attempt to find temporary holding areas and vantage points from which to ambush patrolling pike.

Points or spits of land jutting out into the lake are very obvious starting points on any stillwater. Normally they are great spots for the pike angler to offer his baits at varying depths and distances and cover a substantial area of water. Moreover, patrolling pike following a set depth contour will normally come close in to the bank if there is a sharp drop-off from the point.

On one Norfolk gravel pit I used to fish regularly, the best point swim offered up to 27 feet of water within easy casting distance as well as a shallow, weedy bar and an extensive area of sunken trees on a sharp drop-off. That swim produced a lot of good pike in its early days, but its very obvious nature meant it was frequented too often by other pike anglers. The stage was eventually reached when the lake's pike were clearly avoiding the area.

Like the good matchman or bream angler, the piker should get to know his swim before he starts firing baits out. At the very least, plumb the depth of the areas you are considering casting to to locate the position of underwater shelves and humps. Placing a bait close to such a feature could produce ten times more runs and fish than another bait positioned ten yards further away.

On the pit I just mentioned, Neville Fickling and myself spent a Sunday afternoon out in a boat with an echo-sounder to draw an accurate underwater contour map of the fishery. It was work which paid great dividends, for our subsequent visits produced some excellent pike to 24¼ lb.

Believe me, pike love the cover offered by steep underwater shelves, and will usually follow such pronounced contours when they are out on the prowl. Placing your baits in the right positions will intercept them when they are actively feeding and you will reap the benefits accordingly.

Finding suitable physical features on your typical stillwater is the first step in locating the pike, but it's not enough in itself. Structure fishing, as the Americans call it, can only be the means to identifying the areas the pike are likely to be in—it doesn't mean you're guaranteed to catch.

To shorten the odds yet further, the pike angler should also ensure that his chosen ambush areas are favoured by the resident shoals of fodder fish in the venue. Ask the matchmen and pleasure anglers which are the best swims for, say, bream and roach and you can be fairly sure that the best pike swims won't be too far away.

Note that I *didn't* say the best bream and roach swims would also be the best pike swims; in my experience they are not. Although predator and prey frequently rub shoulders and share the same swim in apparent harmony, it is more usual for the pike to take up residence anything from 20 to 100 yards away.

I can't pretend to understand the mentality of pike, but I get the impression that they like to rest up between active feeding spells within sight, sound and scent of their prey.

In the absence of reliable information from fellow anglers as to the whereabouts of the prey species, the budding pike angler should be prepared to do his own groundwork. Get down to the waterside at the crack of dawn and at dusk to observe the areas where shoals of fish are topping. Use binoculars if necessary and remember that on most venues the bream

First time lucky: Graham Billing took this 30 lb 5 oz lough pike on his very first day in Ireland.

tend to show at the surface early in the morning, while roach prime in earnest between sunset and dusk. Either way, these two species will normally betray their presence at the surface in all but the most hostile of weather conditions.

Bream can be a little unreliable in this context, as rolling bream are also patrolling bream on many occasions and could therefore be some distance from the swims where they are likely to while away most of the day and night. But they should not be too difficult to track down.

Incidentally, I mention roach and bream in the context of prey fish purely because they are the prevalent fodder species on most stillwater pike fisheries. That is not to say that pike prefer roach and bream to all else, merely that the successful opportunist predator feeds upon whatever is most freely available. If your venue is low on stocks of bream, but contains plenty of chub, tench, perch, rudd, small carp or whatever, don't worry—the pike will be more than pleased to eat them.

In searching out pike, most anglers are aware of the importance of finding the right depth, and most autumn and winter pikers seem to elect to fish in around 12 to 13 feet of water when such a depth is available. But although those anglers are giving thought to the depth of the swim they intend to fish, they frequently fail to consider at what depth they should present their bait. The angler fishing in 12 feet of water will usually have his baits hard on the bottom or within a couple of feet of bottom ... even though any pike present could well be suspended two feet below the surface.

That's all well and fine—pike spend a great deal of their time living and feeding at or near the bottom. But it's also a fact that the same pike feed very frequently in midwater and at the surface. The new breed of plug-fishing lure anglers seems to recognise and take advantage of this, but seldom the static angler with his live and deadbaits.

Just pull a surface plug or shallow-running lure through your pike water on the right day and you'll soon forget those daft ideas of pike being bottom feeders. Once you've spent a little time on the bankside you'll also note the frequent occasions on which pike strike at food near the surface—and not just during the warmer months, either.

I well remember the first time I got the opportunity to fish Leisure Sport's superb Thorpe Park gravel pit complex in Surrey. It was a very frosty December morning—the margins of the lake were in fact frozen—but Eddie Turner and myself were still brimming with confidence as we made our way to our chosen pitch, laden down with buckets of trout livebaits and an assortment of deadbaits. We'd heard of Thorpe Park's

Autumn gold: Dave Phillips with a fine pike from a small Fenland drain.

Troller's delight: 16½ lb of muscular Irish pike, which took a trolled plug.

Going back: Dave Phillips returns a big boat-caught pike.

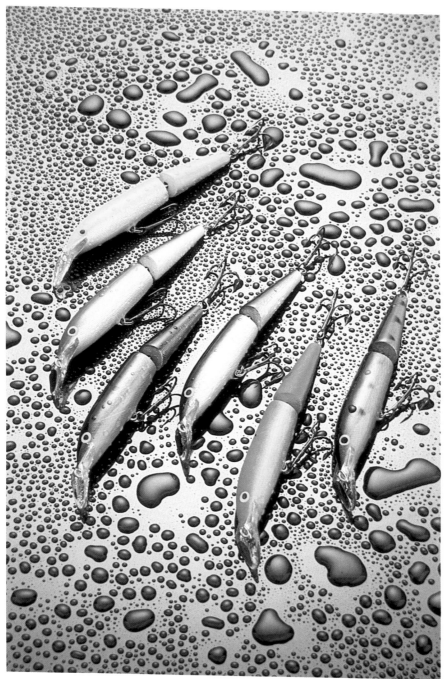

Deadly: Balsa jointed minnow lures.

Spoon-fed: The writer prepares to unhook a small Irish pike.

Fighting-fit: A muscular lough pike.

Fen tiger: Nige Williams returns a 27 lb-plus specimen to its drain home.

Piking afloat: The writer's boat, launched and prepared for a day's lure fishing on a large lake.

Oh Gord: Lancashire pike ace Gord Burton with a useful plug-caught pike.

Continental tastes: This big Finnish pike accepted a small plug bait.

Eastern promise: A Norfolk gravel pit produced this 20lb-plus pike, which fell for a float-legered herring.

Fast Eddie: This reservoir 30-pounder is just one of an incredible string of mega-pike landed by Hertfordshire angler Eddie Turner.

reputation and we were out to do the business!

Setting up two rods apiece, I elected to fish a paternostered livebait and a legered deadbait, while Eddie fished one rod on the paternoster and the other with a free-swimming livebait presented in midwater. Within ten minutes he had banked three pike, including an 18-pounder, on the free-swimming rig, while the other rods hadn't produced a single take. It wasn't very long before I too rigged up a float-fished trout set to swim in midwater ... and by midday I landed over 100 lb of pike, including six in double figures and a 24¼ lb beauty. The paternostered and legered baits were virtually ignored.

There are no hard-and-fast rules in piking, but there are some general trends which suggest what depths produce most pike in varying conditions. We'll look at them later in the book, along with the rigs required to extract the pike from the depth levels at which they are feeding. In the meantime, just bear in mind that locating pike is essentially a three-dimensional exercise.

So far we have only considered stillwaters— namely pits and pools— and have discussed how to find the pike therein. These venues certainly produce most of the better pike caught in this country, but I feel it is only because the majority of pike anglers spend most of their time fishing such waters. I'd now like to turn my attention to other types of venues which also show excellent potential, but in many cases are largely neglected.

Rivers are the obvious candidates for the accolade of the most underused pike angling resource in the country. Despite the very big authenticated river pike taken in the past, most modern anglers seem to pass them by.

Rivers can be a daunting proposition to the angler more used to the sedentary lifestyle of stillwater fishing, but the rewards to be reaped can be terrific. River pike feed hard and fight hard—remember they have the flow of the river to fight against all the time—and they really are a joy to catch.

If you plan to take up river fishing, do yourself a favour and forget the brolly, bedchair and electronic alarms. Travel as light as possible, with a minimum of tackle and baits, and approach your chosen river in the manner of an intelligent, footloose chub angler. Wander from swim to swim, fishing the areas you feel are likely to hold pike, and gradually a pattern will begin to emerge. You'll discover, for example, that sunken trees and bays off the main current are normally excellent holding areas, especially when the river is fining down after a winter flood.

Echo sounder: Invaluable for mapping out the contours of new waters.

You'll also learn that the pike will be out in the main flow more often than you expected—in the sort of swims you'd never expect to find the so-called lazy predator of ambush. That's because pike need to feed to survive, and if the chub and dace are out there in the current, the feeding pike will be there too. They don't grow to 20 lb-plus by sitting in slacks waiting for sick and dying prey to get washed in!

Location of pike, you see, is essentially an exercise in logic. We know that the pike eats other fish, so we need to present a bait in its larder. On the river, we'll therefore concentrate on the areas where the prey species are to be found.

As rivers vary so much in character—from the fast and powerful spate rivers of the north to the sluggish water courses of East Anglia—it is impossible to state categorically where the best river pike swims will be found. Personally, I love lots of features to choose from, for these give the thinking angler a head start.

Finding pike on a featureless stretch of river can be a boring exercise. The time-honoured technique of leap-frogging the rods along the bank until a pack of feeding pike is found is hardly a test of mental agility, but with no variations in depth or flow etc, the piker has little choice.

However, the river with lots of features allows the pike angler to draw a mental image of where the pike will be—and it's always very satisfying to be proved right in the shape of a good pike from the swim you just *knew* would hold one.

As I said earlier, the successful river man should travel like the wandering chub angler—searching out the best lies and ignoring the barren-looking swims. You don't need to carry lots of tackle— in fact anything more than one or two rods and the very minimum of baits and gear is likely to hinder your success.

The very best pike anglers I have ever fished with are all what I would term thinking anglers. They are also working anglers. Never content to fall asleep behind electronic alarms, they are forever looking for a new approach or new area from which to extract pike. If at the end of a long winter's day of pike fishing you are not physically and mentally exhausted, you have probably not been trying hard enough!

Use your imagination: try to visualise where the pike will be on your water on any given day and fish there—even if the swim is a long walk from the car park. And keep trying until you find the pike, for it is a very rare day when no pike at all are willing to feed at some stage. Work hard at attempting to locate the pike and you'll reap the rewards of experience, for eventually you'll be more often right than wrong.

Pleasure park pike: This 24 lb 4 oz pike was the best of a big haul of specimens taken during a hectic morning at Thorpe Park in Surrey.

Fig. 12. Big pike country: Norfolk's River Thurne, which has produced monsters to over 40 lb.

The great thing about pike fishing, of course, is great variety of waters capable of producing specimen fish. Throughout lowland Britain, the pike is the major predator on all our freshwater fisheries and is capable of growing to a good size in any venue with sufficient stocks of food.

I was born and bred in Norfolk's Fenland, with the drains of my home county as well as north Cambridgeshire and south Lincolnshire within easy striking distance. These man-made waterways suffered some setbacks a few years ago due to poor spawning by the resident roach and bream, but their recovery in recent years has been nothing short of amazing.

There are some very big pike for the taking on even the most insignificant-looking Fen drains and many anglers from all over the country are again making the pilgrimage eastwards to fish them. Among them is my old mate Eddie Turner, who was fortunate enough to catch a 30 lb-plus pike I had seen lying in the shallows—and not feeding!— on a previous trip.

Also in East Anglia, the Broads are still worth a try, especially now that the commercial boating interests are taking a more responsible stance towards this unique wetland environment. There are thousands of acres of rich, productive pike water in the Broads system and despite the problems the area has suffered in the past, I reckon recent developments will see even better pike fishing in this region.

Not everybody has access to fishing of that calibre, of course, but there are still some surprises to be had in most areas. Few anglers in the Midlands fish the extensive canal systems for pike, but there are one or two useful specimens to be had. The Grand Union Canal near Newport Pagnell has produced pike to over 25 lb in recent seasons, yet receives virtually no pressure from pike anglers.

And there are always the reservoirs. One of my angling mates, Graham Billing, has specialised in pike fishing on the Midlands reservoirs and has taken some excellent pike from several of the region's big still-waters. Graham and one or two other pikers from the Northampton area have taken apart waters like the moody Stanford Reservoir and demonstrated just how productive these big stillwaters can be.

Mind you, Graham's biggest claim to fame came on his very first trip to Ireland. His first run on his first day in the Emerald Isle produced a 30 lb-plus monster! There is no doubt that the Irish and Scottish waters are full of potential; even the numbers of dedicated English pikers who make their pilgrimages to the loughs and lochs every close season have hardly scratched the surface of these inland seas.

Don't neglect any venue in your quest for big pike. Natural pools, estate lakes and even over-sized farm ponds are all capable of yielding specimen fish provided they are rich and have sufficient stocks of fodder fish to provide the pike with a suitable diet.

There are big pike out there ready to be caught. Avoid the crowds and think for yourself and you could well discover a dream pike fishery that is unfished by other pike anglers. I have no doubt that there are yet waters to find that will surpass even Llandegfedd Reservoir.

Don't forget — discarded line kills birds and other wild animals

When To Go

Having looked at location and learned where to go pike fishing, it's now time to consider when to go piking—and how weather and water conditions affect our prospects.

Traditionally, the autumn and winter months were considered the time for pike anglers to ply their trade. In fact until comparatively recently, many areas of the country did not allow pike fishing until October 1. This abbreviated pike season was imperative in years gone by because most pike were killed for the pot, and this was still the case until about two decades ago when a more enlightened breed of angler appeared on the scene. These days, although pike killing does still exist in isolated areas of the country, the vast majority of anglers are conservation-conscious and return their pike as a matter of course.

There is, therefore, no justifiable moral argument against pike fishing right through from June 16 to March 14. But is it worth it?

The answer, simply, is yes. Although most of my pike fishing in the past was conducted through the colder months, I am these days more appreciative of warm-water piking, particularly since I got more involved in fishing artificial baits. In fact now, with regular close season forays to the Irish loughs (there is no coarse fish close season for pike in Eire), I actually enjoy quality pike fishing 12 months of the year.

If pounds and ounces are your game above all else, then there is a logical argument which suggests fishing for pike before Christmas would be a waste of time. It cannot be denied that specimen pike do weigh considerably lighter after they have spawned (usually between the middle of March and the middle of April) and don't really pack the weight back on until early in the New Year when the roe (all big pike are females) starts to develop. But the angler who avoids all but spawn-laden pike would be missing out on some excellent sport.

Catching pike in the summer isn't always an easy business. The fish are certainly more widely dispersed than they are in the colder months and a static sit-and-wait approach is not as effective as it is in winter when you know you are in a prime swim. But this is hardly an effective argument when the best fun of all in the warmer weather is to set out light, with lure tackle, and search out the pike. Warm-water pike will often provide you with explosive action to surface baits and will certainly fight harder than their winter counterparts.

The pike's fighting ability in warm weather is likely to leave the angler quite exhausted: a five-minute scrap from a modest double-figure pike is by no means out of the question and can quite often leave the muscles in your rod arm aching. But remember, too, that the pike will be even more tired than the angler and should be unhooked and returned to the water as quickly as possible. In no circumstances should pike be put in keepnets or sacks in warm weather, as the sun-warmed shallows of the water are likely to have little or no dissolved oxygen and could, therefore, kill your quarry. And don't get involved in David Bailey-style photo sessions of your catch in hot or windy weather, even if your pike is a big one. Its slime will dry out incredibly quickly in the sun and breeze and your activities could again leave you with a dead pike on your hands. A quick snapshot and rapid return to the water is the order of the day.

Similarly, the summer is no time for light-line heroics. We all know that lines of 8 lb or less will eventually tire a big pike in all but the snaggiest of swims, but what has the angler proved? Only an incompetent would lose a battle against even a big pike on such tackle, so there is no point of prolonging the battle and causing distress to the fish. There is nothing 'sporting' about playing a good pike to a dangerous level of exhaustion or, worse, snapping off and letting it swim away to a slow death because its mouth was sealed with a set of treble hooks. I never go down below 11 lb line for any form of pike fishing—and I step up to 12, 15 or even 18 lb line when the circumstances demand.

Some anglers are disappointed by summer pike fishing because they treat it much the same as their winter piking—i.e. pitched up with brolly and bedchair, and legered deadbaits left to fester on the bottom of the swim. It's about as action-packed as fishing for double-figure bream and, possibly, demonstrates a certain laziness on the part of the angler.

Static summer deadbaiting is a slow game. As we have already seen, summer pike are active feeders and, on most waters, prefer a moving target. There are exceptions, but generally I would expect warm-weather pike to respond best to artificials or livebaits. I prefer artificials—mainly because they are effective, but also because livebaits find it so difficult

Frosty reception: Cambridgeshire angler John Ward lured this 26 lb pike from a hole in the ice on a local gravel pit.

to live up to their name in warm weather and actually stay alive.

Fishing for pike in the spring in Ireland and Scotland has taught me that they do feed hard after spawning, with late April and early May being particularly good for big hauls of hungry pike. This feeding pattern appears to continue through into June and, indeed, the first couple of weeks of the English open season are usually very good for pike. Results do tend to drop off in midsummer on most waters—generally, because heavy weed growth tends to make bait presentation difficult. Again, the thoughtful use of artificial lures at such times will go some way to eliminating the problem; at the very least the pike angler can cover a lot of water and stand a chance of presenting a bait to several feeding pike in the course of a session.

One of the biggest problems in summer piking, however, has to be the level of energy expended by the angler. Dawn-to-dusk sessions in winter are all well and fine when there is just seven hours of daylight to contend with, but 18-hour roving sessions in the heat of the summer are too much for me! Right through the warmer months, I try to restrict piking sessions to a few hours here and there—generally early in the morning or late in the evening.

As I said earlier, pike do seem to be less localised in the summer, and I feel this is probably because their prey are generally more active and dispersed throughout the fishery. This situation, however, normally changes as autumn appears.

Once the first night frosts arrive and water temperatures start to plummet, the shoals of roach and bream or whatever are likely to pack quite tightly into certain areas of the fishery. This is particularly true of the current year's fry, which really do form dense shoals. This time of the year—usually late September and on through October—is when the angler can capitalise on ravenous, fry-feeding pike.

Make no mistake about it: on many fisheries the pike will feed as avidly on fry as a group of carp on a rich bloodworm bed. And they can be just as preoccupied at times, ignoring sizeable livebaits in favour of a mouthful of tiny 1–1½ inch roach. Happily, they will more often accept anything on offer during their feeding frenzy, so don't be too surprised to land a decent pike on a half-mackerel bait and discover, upon unhooking it, that it is already stuffed to the gill rakers with fry.

Fry-feeding pike will often betray their presence by crashing into the fry shoals on the surface, causing quite spectacular boils and swirls. This can happen over deep water as well as shallow areas ... and it is the signal for the pike angler to move his baits into the area quickly!

Fen record: Martin Geraghty with his incredible 34 lb 4 oz drain pike. It measured
a full 47 inches long!

It is interesting to debate whether the shoals of fry are packed tightly
because they have been herded into position by a pack of pike, or whether
the pike have simply moved in to take advantage of a situation that
already exists. I believe the latter to be the case, although on several
occasions I have come across a shoal of small fish surrounded by pike
and, apparently, trapped. Either way, early autumn is the time to look
out for this situation and get a lot of pike under your belt: big catches
are certainly on the cards.

These packs of pike can consist of individual fish of all sizes, apparently living in close harmony, although at times you may strike into a
succession of big pike or jacks. But even if big pike are your game and
you are catching small pike one after the other, don't move swims to
avoid them—the next take could be from a 20 lb-plus specimen! I can
recall at least two occasions when successive casts to the same swim have
produced a micro-pike of less than 1 lb followed closely by a meaty 20-
pounder!

In the above cases it is obvious the larger pike concerned could
have quite happily tackled their smaller brethren—but didn't. Just
how bite-sized jacks can at times live in close harmony with big pike is a

phenomenon I can't explain—no more than I would pretend to under-stand why small pike will sometimes tackle specimen fish of their own size.

I well remember fishing from a boat with John Watson on Martham Broad in Norfolk in January 1983, just before the word got out and hordes of anglers descended on the area in search of specimen pike. We had arrived in darkness, moored up behind a dense reedbed to escape the attentions of passing boats on the nearby River Thurne, and were fishing legered deadbaits into a small area of very shallow water.

Within minutes of first light, John's legered chub bait was away and he quickly boated a pike of just under 20 lb that was literally lacerated by fresh teethmarks from a pike with a jaw size that I certainly hadn't been fortunate enough to encounter in the past.

'Eh-up, there's 40-pounders in here,' whispered John ... just as my legered smelt was picked up by another double-figure pike. This fish, upon inspection, had been savaged so badly in the distant past that the wound on its underside had healed leaving a fold of its gut trapped outside its body! It was in perfect health though, so I returned it quickly to the water ... although I was careful not to leave my fingers dangling over the side of the boat for too long!

Anyway, I digress. The fact is that despite the hazards sometimes encountered from greedy pack members, pike do stick together more or less throughout the winter. I'm sure the shoals thus formed have a fairly loose arrangement, with members breaking away from the informal group from time to time, but some individual pike do seem to be insepar-able. In the autumn of 1982, when Martin Geraghty and myself were having a tremendous run of good pike on a short stretch of a fenland drain, there were two pike—a 16-pounder and a 10 lb specimen—which would often put in an appearance at the same time, from the same swim. It was almost as though they couldn't bear to be parted and if one was caught the other would take a bait too, just to join it on the bank!

Ironically, the first occasion on which we encountered the toothsome twosome they were included in a spectacular haul of pike of all sizes which was topped by a magnificent 34¼ lb monster to Martin. Suffice it to say *that* one *didn't* turn up again ...

The string of catches Martin and I enjoyed from that hotspot that autumn came in all sorts of weather conditions, although the best times were invariably after a sharp, overnight frost. As soon as the rising sun appeared over the flat fenland horizon, the runs would start coming and the pike would generally continue to feed until around 9 am when the sun was quite strong. Interestingly, when the weather was dour and we

Border line: The River Wye on the English–Welsh border is a great pike river, but winter floods often rule it out.

fished in the wind and rain, the runs would be fewer and later—with mid-morning seeing the best of the action.

That same drain tended to be quite dour during midwinter, but would invariably produce the goods again in the last few weeks of the season. By then, however, afternoons would produce the majority of big fish— especially during mild weather.

It is difficult to give advice on weather conditions for piking, simply because so many waters respond differently to various conditions. As a general rule, I would fish very confidently on most waters in winter during periods of high atmospheric pressure—even when those climatic conditions had produced clear skies and very hard overnight frosts. At such times I have even taken pike to over 20 lb from holes in the ice!

High pressure in autumn and the back end of the season can also produce thick fog—which is also a blessing to my mind as long as it is not *freezing* fog. I have heard other anglers decry foggy weather as an ill omen for pike catches, but I've certainly found the reverse to be true, with some waters producing their very best results in such conditions. In fact my biggest fenland pike (25 lb 14 oz) came to the bank among a sizeable haul of good fish in February 1980 during a real pea-souper.

Experiments carried out by Barrie Rickards and friends over a number of years appeared to demonstrate that big pike showed a preference to livebaits and artificial lures during periods of high pressure and a rising barometer. Conversely, they found on their waters that times of low pressure were those when static deadbaits were most likely to succeed.

That evidence was arrived at following the capture of a very large number of pike and calculated on a sound scientific basis, so I'm not about to challenge it. I will state, however, that in my experience on the waters I have fished, periods of high pressure also produce better catches of pike to deadbaits *on those venues where deadbaiting is generally the most effective method.*

The truth of the matter is that few of us are able to pick and choose our fishing days—and we have to contend with whatever the weather decides to throw at us during our winter outings. Happily there are no hard-and-fast rules governing pike behaviour and very big pike have the pleasant habit of turning up in even the most adverse conditions. Long may it remain so!

On stillwaters, one of the most difficult periods of the year for piking is when the water temperatures really plummet down to just above freezing point. This normally happens around Christmas most winters and the pike seem to become very dour at this time. Being cold-blooded creatures, the pike probably undergo quite a shock at such times, so I suppose their reluctance to go on a feeding rampage is quite understandable.

However, within a week or so the pike normally recover from the trauma and will often be prepared to feed quite freely, even though water temperatures are still rock-bottom. My first instinct at such times is to fish very deep water—20 feet or more—although the pike don't necessarily agree with my instincts and will quite often be located in much shallower areas!

On stillwaters an inflowing stream might be pushing warmer water into the lake and, therefore, be creating an attractive area for both prey and pike. On the other hand it might be awash with melted snow-water . . . which is the only thing I know guaranteed to kill all angling prospects on all waters.

Of course, snow-water is the biggest problem for the winter river piker. I dearly love big rivers like the Herefordshire Wye, which to my mind simply screams out big pike, but I know that, for much of the winter, water conditions rule it out.

The Wye, like most of our remaining *natural* rivers, receives much

Night feeder: Neville Fickling nabbed this 18 lb pike as darkness fell on a Norfolk gravel pit. He went on to take several more nocturnal pike from this venue.

of its water from high ground—in this case the Welsh hills. And when snow on the high ground thaws, the meltwater pours into the river, causing even the hungry chub to lose their appetites. Even mild weather produces its problems in the form of floodwater and I can assure the reader that a river carrying 14 feet of dirty-brown water and assorted flotsam is no place to expect a good catch of pike.

Like other types of venue, most rivers appear to fish well after a sharp overnight frost—so long as the river is not very low and clear. I reckon the best general conditions on the majority of rivers I have fished in winter are a combination of mild weather and fairly clear water. In fact catch the river when it has been fining down for a few days after a flood and you could be in business.

Lucky pike anglers who live near chalk-fed rivers have, of course, got it made. Unlike the spate-type rivers we have just discussed, these venues don't suffer the same extremes of floods etc and are therefore more consistent. The high pH of chalk streams also ensures a healthy food chain and, all things being equal, meaty great pike at the head of the chain! Wessex rivers like the Hampshire Avon and Dorset Stour have long sustained justified reputations as first-class pike fisheries and still produce specimens of over 30 lb most seasons, despite the well-documented decline in fishing for other species, particularly on the once-proud Avon.

As you may have gathered by now, the versatile pike angler with access to different types of venue can usually enjoy quality pike fishing throughout the worst extremes of the British weather, provided he puts some thought into his choice of water. Even the freak sub-Arctic conditions we experience every few years needn't deter you if you live within travelling distance of a warm-water outflow. Early in 1987, when the country was in the grip of a severe freeze-up, I headed for the River Trent below the power station outfalls at Nottingham ... and was rewarded with a stack of hard-fighting river pike to double figures.

Times of year and day, and weather conditions, all have a big part to play in pike fishing and the angler who understands them will certainly be well-equipped to catch his share of pike. But before I round off this chapter, there is one more factor to consider—and that is nocturnal pike.

Pike *do* feed after dark on most waters—and evidence so far suggests they feed regularly after nightfall on fisheries which are hammered by anglers during the daylight hours. Shallow, clear waters which see a lot of daytime activity from boats and other water users—like certain areas of the Norfolk Broads—are also proving to be effective targets for the pike angler prepared to put in the hours after nightfall.

It is all very interesting and certainly demonstrates the pioneering attitude of the new generation of pike anglers, but I have to admit that these days all-night sessions in the depths of winter don't appeal to me when I can enjoy daytime sport on other waters. My nocturnal piking activities these days are restricted to an hour before first light and an hour or more after nightfall—both of which can be very productive periods on most venues.

I'd be the last person to decry the piking night-owls—I admire any angler prepared to put up with considerable discomfort in his quest for fish—but I'm afraid they're not for me!

Tackle

As the reader will have already gathered, pike fishing is a specialised sport which requires a single-minded approach. It also requires some specialised items of tackle. Luckily for today's pike angler, modern tackle manufacturers produce a wide range of excellent tailor-made products—a far cry from the situation as little as ten years ago, when the keen piker was obliged to build much of his own kit.

Setting up your stall as a pike angler couldn't be easier . . . or could it? The fact is that the newcomer can easily find himself bewildered by the range of specialised pike tackle available and beguiled by the seductive advertising and hype. State-of-the-art carbon rods costing upwards of £100 truly are a delight to use, but in all honesty are unlikely to repay your investment in terms of bigger and better catches. Likewise, today there are excellent fixed spool reels available for £20 that are better value than some costing treble the price.

In this context, liken fishing tackle to motor cars. It is possible to buy a sound, reliable second-hand vehicle for £1,000 or less and it will get you from A to B in much the same manner as a fuel-injected modern beast costing £15,000 or more. But you are more likely to enjoy the experience of travelling in the latter. Likewise, owning and using first-class tackle is likely to enhance your enjoyment at the waterside.

There is no doubt that many of the items of tackle on display at your local dealer fall into the luxury bracket, but on the other hand some pieces of gear can be classed as essentials. For example, it is imperative to use wire traces on all occasions when pike fishing. Even very small pike have great mouthfuls of needle-sharp teeth which will cut through nylon monofilament in a very short time. Looking inside a pike's open mouth would give a dentist nightmares—there are hundreds of backward-facing rows of teeth everywhere. Even the roof of the jaw and the tongue are covered in teeth.

To avoid your contact with a fish of a lifetime being a fleeting one, ensure you use good-quality wire trace material at all times. I have used various brands over the years, but right now I use Peter Drennan's trace wire; not because it is any better than Marlinsteel and twisted Alasticum etc, but simply because it is easy to obtain from any local tackle shop. Avoid nylon-covered wire and single-strand Alasticum as trace materials as neither are as strong and supple as premium multi-strand stainless steel wire.

For general pike fishing, my traces consist of about 15 inches of wire with a breaking strain of 15–20 lb. To one end I attach a Berkley swivel of 50–60 lb BS, while two strong treble hooks, normally size 8 or 10, are attached to the other. For fishing artificial lures I use traces nine inches long, with a Berkley or ball bearing swivel attached at one end and a snaplock fitting at the other.

Whatever trace wire you use, check it regularly for kinking. A kink in wire reduces its breaking strain to next to nothing, with the obvious outcome if a big pike is hooked.

Treble hooks are a personal choice. I have no firm favourites, for I have tried many patterns and found very few unsatisfactory. I'm not a great fan of barbless hooks, because there was no doubt I did lose more hooked fish when I gave them an extended trial some years back. Instead, I prefer to file down the barbs somewhat to leave a small, reduced barb on each point of the treble. And I always carry a sharpening stone to keep the points very keen for maximum penetration.

Most tackle shops carry a selection of treble hooks from Mustad, Partridge, Peter Drennan and Eagle Claw. All of those brands are very good indeed, but it is wise to check each hook individually before use just to ensure that a dud hasn't slipped through the factory's quality control net.

Line for pike fishing is another area where the angler must be very vigilant, for it is the line more than anything else that suffers when big baits are being cast and sizeable specimens are being hooked and landed. Abrasive gravel bars, mussel beds and snags like sunken branches are also very injurious to nylon monofilament.

These days I am very conservative in my line choice: I use bulk spools of Sylcast mono for all my pike fishing. Sylcast is the most abrasion-resistant line I have ever used, it is very reliable and has enough stretch to cushion the sudden rushes made by a sizeable hard-fighting fish. Moreover, it is very reasonably-priced, which means I can afford to change the line of all my spools at least once every two months throughout the pike season. This may sound rather extravagant, but there is no doubt

Weatherbeaten: But Dave is more than pleased with this 26½ lb pike, taken on carbon rod and fixed-spool reel outfit on a southern reservoir.

that nylon monofilament deteriorates quite rapidly once exposed to sunlight, immersed in water and subjected to the strain of casting and playing fish. I use it in 11 lb breaking strain for general piking, stepping up to 15 lb or even 18 lb in snaggy situations, or lure fishing around extensive weedbeds in the summer months.

Although it is possible, at a pinch, to press other rods into service for pike fishing, you will be a lot more comfortable if you acquire the proper tools for the job. Personally, I tend to err on the heavy side when I am choosing my own rods and prefer to use through-action tools of around 3 lb test curve in most situations. These rods are very powerful—capable of casting heavy baits long distances—and are more than a match for any pike swimming in British waters. But many pike anglers prefer lighter rods for their general piking, opting for test curves of between 2–2½ lb. A rod along these lines is certainly very acceptable for most piking requirements, but not really capable of sending heavy baits like half mackerel to the horizon!

If you do a little carp fishing, it is possible that you already have a couple of rods in the 2 lb test curve class. If so, you will certainly be able to put a few pike on the bank; at one time I often used a 1½ lb test Mark IV carp rod for livebaiting in the Fens and I succeeded in landing a number of pike to over 20 lb on it. These lighter rods are okay at a pinch, but I wouldn't risk a light carbon carp rod for pike fishing. The old glass rods I used to use were forgiving beasts and accepted a degree of over-loading without complaint, but carbon fibre is a less tolerant material and will not take the sort of abuse we used to dish out to our rods 15 years ago! If you insist on casting heavy pike baits on light carbon wands, you'll wind up with a splintered rod on your hands.

However, there is no doubt that today's specialist carbon pike rods are far superior to the heavy old glass rods we all used ten years ago. Carbon fibre is an excellent material and well worth considering provided you don't expect your carbon rod to exceed the purpose it was designed for.

I prefer rods at least ten feet long, and preferably about 11 feet in length. Through-action rods are best, for most of the baits we cast are heavy but not particularly dense. Only when casting small baits on big leads does the pike angler need to resort to fast-taper, tip-actioned rods.

In the past, it was possible to keep the costs down by building your own pike rods. Some manufacturers still supply full kits with all the materials you need to build your own first-class rods, but cut-throat competition between tackle companies and cheap labour in the Far East means that there is little to save these days by building your own. However, it can be a lot of fun on a winter's evening for the DIY fan who yearns to possess his own custom-built rods.

Handles and reel fittings are a matter of choice and, personally, I'm not too fussy which I have on my rods, provided they are secure and the reel can be fixed about 24 inches up from the butt. But if you intend using multipliers for your pike work, ensure that you use rods with screw or clip-type reel fittings, as the old sliding winch fittings are totally unsuitable.

I seldom use multiplier reels unless I am lure fishing, in which case I also use specialised baitcasting rods, which are designed to be fished with the reel positioned on top of the handle. My armoury of lure rods comes from Abu and ranges from a tiny 7½ ft wand for casting small plugs up to a 10 ft double-handed job employed for casting big lures and trolling big waters from a boat. I prefer using multipliers and lighter rods for general lure fishing because casting is easier and more accurate, as well as being a lot less tiring during a long summer session. However, the newcomer to artificials would be advised to use a standard fixed spool outfit until he is certain he intends to do a lot of lure fishing.

On the subject of reels, it has to be admitted that the fixed spool is certainly the most versatile tool for the pike angler. I have also taken double-figure fish on a closed-face, various multipliers and a centre-pin, but I would be the first to admit that a good fixed spool is better in most circumstances.

These days, there is a wide choice of models from many manufacturers, but remember to use reels with a spool large enough to take at least 150 yards of 11 lb line. More expensive models will boast extra features—some of which are totally unnecessary—and the better ones will normally boast a wider-than-average spool and superior line-lay. The latter is very important, for there are few angling experiences more irritating than finding the coils of line on your reel have bedded into themselves while playing in a big, dour fish ... when all you want to do is cast out quickly to the same spot in the hope of *another* big, dour fish!

My favourite reels are from the Mitchell and Abu stables, although I wouldn't be parted from the tiny Ryobi multiplier I use when tackling summer pike with my light baitcasting outfit.

Fill your reels to within 3 mm of the brim, taking care not to put excessive twist into the line when transferring it from line spool to reel spool. When loading a fixed spool reel, the line should come off the end

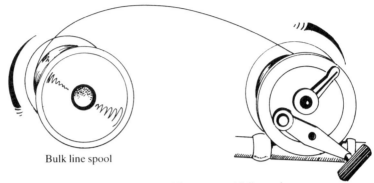

Bulk line spool

Correct loading of line onto multiplier reel

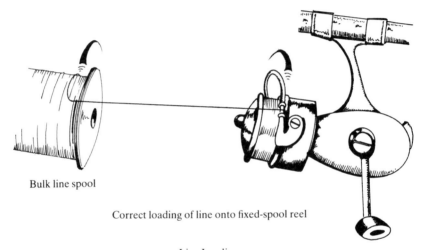

Bulk line spool

Correct loading of line onto fixed-spool reel

Line Loading.

of the line spool in the same direction as the rotation of the bale arm. On multipliers, let the line spool rotate (see diagrams).

Having dealt with the tackle basics, it's now time to look at the other specialised tools the piker uses, some of which are essential and others worth having just to make life easier.

Essentials include a good set of long-nosed artery forceps for unhooking your catch. We'll discuss unhooking techniques later, but for now let me assure you that nothing compares with forceps for safe removal of hooks in pike fishing. The specialised pike disgorgers now available do work, but they are fiddly and cumbersome in practice and, in the wrong hands, can cause untold damage to the pike.

Similarly, anglers fishing on gravel pits and reservoirs can make a mess of the pike they catch by unhooking them on hard or rough surfaces. If there is no soft grass in the immediate area, you should always unhook your pike on a suitable soft synthetic surface. The Unhooking Mat, marketed by ET Products, is ideal for this purpose and should be carried by caring pike anglers at all times.

It's no secret that the shining light behind ET Products is top pike angler Eddie Turner—the man who has landed more 30 lb-plus pike than any other angler in the history of the sport. Eddie's inventiveness and flair have resulted in a host of quality products that many of today's pike enthusiasts swear by. These include the Backbiter electronic drop-off alarms, sunken and standard pike floats, drifters, sacks and pike tubes. It is well worth checking out the range when you are shopping for tried and tested accessories. As far as I'm concerned, if it carries the ET logo it's the best.

Again, the enthusiastic DIY man can have some fun with balsa wood, glue and paint making his own floats etc. But I would advise against making your own drop-off electronic alarms unless you are a very competent electronics man. It is imperative that bite indication in pike fishing is totally reliable—the failure of an audible alarm can result in a deeply-hooked fish. And a pike hooked deeply can very easily become a dead one.

What else will you need? Well, the average angler about to turn his attention to the pike is likely to already own a brolly, rod rests, holdall and chair. Most pike anglers seem to enjoy the home comforts and many actually set up a mini-camp whenever they go fishing, sleeping on the comfort of a carp-style bedchair under the brolly while waiting for their audible alarms to tell them a pike has picked up their baits.

I have to admit, however, that this style of pike fishing is not for me. Indeed, you won't catch me dead with a brolly unless there is a strong likelihood of torrential rain. If there is a long walk involved to my favoured swims and I want to stay mobile for the day, I won't even bother with a chair. The sedentary pike angler isn't usually the most effective angler on the waterside. When I want to sleep, I tuck myself under the duvet in the comfort of my own bedroom; when I fish I concentrate on the job in hand and put in some mental and physical effort. At the end of a day's fishing I get a lot more satisfaction knowing I have earned what I have caught.

And the odds are that I will have caught considerably more than the dozing dozens around me. A prime example of the increased catch rate enjoyed by the active, thinking pike angler can be found on one of my local reservoirs, which has the reputation of being a 'hard' water. This particular venue has been very kind to myself and one or two friends, but I am not exaggerating when I say that some anglers think themselves lucky if they get a run a month while fishing there. Those same anglers pick a swim, apparently at random, cast out two rods fastened to electronic alarms and settle down to 'enjoy' a long day of inactivity without any regard to watercraft. I wonder if they ever pause to consider whether the sparse pike population in the venue in question ever come to within a hundred yards of the comfortable base camps they establish for themselves?

On this water the pike are very nomadic in their habits, following the venue's wandering roach shoals and spending much of their time in areas actually out of bounds to anglers. The pike anglers most successful there have been those who have stuck their necks out, made the effort to fish where they believe the pike are . . . and then packed up and moved on again and again until they found them.

This open-minded approach paid dividends to one deserving soul who landed two 30 lb-plus pike in a season from the water by letting the quarry, rather than personal comfort, dictate his approach. One of his big fish actually came from a swim which most anglers regarded as unfishable.

The moral of this tale is don't get too bogged down with non-essential items of tackle on the bank. A mountain of gear does make the prospect of moving from a non-productive swim very daunting and your fishing will suffer as a result. Believe me, the angler who follows his instincts and moves on to a new area of water when he gets 'that' gut feeling will be vindicated enough times to realise that instinct plays a very large part in the location and capture of big pike.

And that is why I try to trim my tackle to the bare essentials whenever I go pike fishing. Waterproof clothing keeps the worst of the winter weather out, provided it is of good quality. Thermal underwear, woollen socks, insulated Skeetex boots and one-piece waxed cotton suits will keep the winter elements at bay, while a rucksack and a Terry Eustace rod quiver is enough to carry all the gear you'll need for a day's piking.

Apart from that, you only have bait storage to worry about. I carry my deadbaits in an insulated cool bag complete with gel freezer blocks, while livebaits are carried in a polythene bin, prior to being transferred

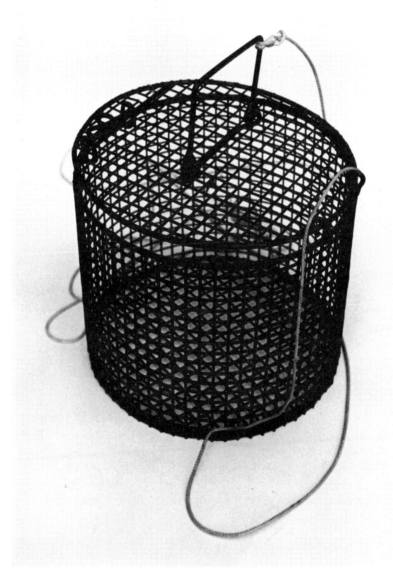

Bait storage: A bait cage like this is ideal for keeping livebaits in perfect condition at your swim.

to an ET Bait Cage on arrival at the swim. The latter, incidentally, is no longer in production, although I understand ET now produces a Bait Tube—a mini-version of the conservation-conscious Pike Tube—for keeping livebaits in perfect condition at the bankside.

If you're a lure fanatic, your bait-storage needs are altogether different. What you require is a box that is easily portable from swim to swim, yet capacious enough to hold a wide selection of baits in a tangle-free state. If you've ever attempted to disentangle a rats' nest of multi-hooked plug lures, you'll know what I mean!

In the past, you'd have had to look towards the USA for a suitable lure box, but the recent upsurge of interest in artificial lures for pike has seen suitable containers become more readily available in the UK. Shakespeare, for example, markets an excellent range of lure boxes at down-to-earth prices that admirably fits the bill. And if you're looking for something a little more extravagant, Normark Sports is currently importing the superb Plano range of boxes—albeit at a price.

And talking of lures brings me to the subject of the last essential item of tackle the pike angler needs—a good landing net. I actually use two—one for lure fishing and one for general pike fishing. The former is a Balcombe Fastnet, a superb fold-down job that is easily transported along the bank, yet can quickly be set up while actually playing fish. This particular model has 36 in. arms and half-inch mesh, which helps to cut down on tangles when a pike is landed and the stray hooks from the lure get entwined in the mesh.

Actually, I very seldom resort to using this net, as I hate the prospect of spending long periods of time removing lures from wet net mesh. Beaching or landing pike by hand is fairly safe and straightforward once you've had a little experience.

Likewise, smaller pike that pick up livebaits and deadbaits seldom grace my other landing net, a triangular 42 in North Western job. But as treble hooks are less likely to be hanging stray in these circumstances, I'm more prepared to get a decent pike in the net and on the bank as quickly as possible.

Once on the bank, our pike is unhooked, weighed and—if big enough—photographed. But those procedures will be discussed later, in the final chapter.

To wind up this chapter, I'll look at one non-essential item of gear that I would be lost without—and that is a boat. The angler used to fishing from terra firma often finds himself decidedly uncomfortable when he first takes to the water in a fishing dinghy, but setting out afloat does

Phone home: A lighter moment on the bankside with ET Products' boss, Eddie
Turner, author of that excellent book, *Mega-Pike.*

literally open up whole new areas to explore, where permitted.

Unfortunately, many clubs and owners do not allow boat fishing on their venues, so the pike angler has to stick to dry land in these circumstances. But where boat fishing is permitted, it is generally far more effective and productive compared to bank fishing. My three largest pike were all taken while fishing afloat, which is particularly significant when one considers that at least 90 per cent of my pike fishing is done from the bank!

Where boat fishing is allowed in this country, there is generally an entrepreneur on hand willing to hire them out to anglers at a reasonable sum. And when that is the case, I certainly don't bother to drag my own boat to the venue and suffer the hassle of handling and launching it.

But my own boat—a 10 ft cathedral-hulled craft which I transport on my car's roof rack and can launch and unload myself—is invaluable when exploring the smaller lakes in Ireland, for example. As I said earlier, I spend quite a lot of time fishing in Ireland during springtime, and since most of Eire's lakes are unfishable from the bank due to bog, bank fishing is out of the question.

Besides, pottering around any water in a boat is a most enjoyable way of pike fishing—and it also opens up the possibility of trolling for pike ... just one of the specialised techniques we'll be looking at in the next chapter.

Tactics

Before going into depth on the tactics used by modern pike anglers, I'd first like to discuss baits. In this chapter I'll be looking at all manner of ways of putting big pike on the bank—using deadbaits, livebaits and artificials. It is up to the individual reader whether he opts out of livebaiting through personal choice.

The same tired old pro- and anti-livebaiting arguments have been raging intensely over the past decade. To my mind it is illogical for anglers to argue that it is cruel to impale a live fish on the hooks for bait, since all anglers go fishing in the hope of impaling their quarry on a hook. To put a moral question mark over the practice of livebaiting effectively says that angling as a whole is cruel.

I use livebaits myself quite often, when necessary to catch pike. I don't use them as much as I did in the past, but that is mainly because I spend so much of my time fishing for pike with artificial baits. I hate the hassle involved in obtaining livebaits, storing them and transporting them ... but there is no doubt that the pike on some waters, on some days, will take virtually nothing else. To suggest that livebaits are unnecessary is to be less than honest.

Over the years I have come to some firm conclusions on baits. There is no doubt, for example, that on most venues livebaits produce more runs than deadbaiting, yielding a smaller average size on account of the numbers of jack pike apparently unwilling to succumb to the delights of a legered deadbait.

However, looking back on my own records, it is interesting to note that my own tally of 20 lb-plus fish shows that they have fallen in equal numbers to both methods.

Meanwhile, artificial lures produce many smaller pike than both livebaiting and deadbaiting, including quite large numbers of micro-pike weighing less than 1 lb apiece. The latter are quite rare catches to livebaits on most venues—and virtually never fall to deadbaits.

Smelt lover: Dave with a personal-best Broads pike of 27½ lb that took a fancy to an unusual deadbait.

But never write off artificial lures as prime baits for big pike. On some venues, particularly big, open waters, lures can produce more specimen pike than more conventional methods—on the right day. Bear in mind that Gareth Edwards' current 45 lb-plus record pike took a Mepps spinner!

Whatever baits you elect to use in your quest for pike, you'll need to employ the correct tactics to present them to the pike and tempt them to take them. Thankfully, a modest repertoire of techniques will suffice to do the business on most occasions. Some of the complicated rigs you read of from time to time in the angling press are devised by armchair anglers who are a lot stronger on practice than theory; I often suspect they invent the rig first then look around for a problem for it to solve.

Of course, some of the new set-ups do serve a purpose. Advances made by anglers like Eddie Turner in perfecting long-range legering and drift float fishing have opened up some great piking opportunities on big waters which, in the past, were difficult to crack. But, generally, three basic rigs will cover all live and deadbaiting eventualities on the vast majority of our venues.

A float-paternoster rig and a leger set-up are my favourite methods on most pike waters—and the pike seem to share the same preference! The float-paternoster is used for livebaits and suspended deadbaits, while the leger is employed for static deadbaits, fished on the bottom.

The third method, the free-roaming float rig, is used for covering more water—or trotting on rivers. Fished just off the bottom, or at mid-water if you feel the pike are active nearer the surface, this set-up is again useful for both livebaits and suspended deadbaits.

To fish a free-roamer, I keep my reel line well greased to keep it floating. For this purpose, I employ an ET Auto Greaser, loaded to the brim with line grease. This ingenious device, fitted inside the butt ring of the rod, coats the line with floatant every time you retrieve and prevents a sinking line from ruining your presentation.

The greased line floats on the surface, while the addition of weight above the trace swivel will keep surface-seeking livebaits down in the water, preventing unwanted tangles. Medium-sized livebaits are generally strong enough to cover water by themselves, but the greased line—aided by surface drift or the faintest breeze—will form into a considerable bow and tow less active baits round in a water-searching arc.

On some days you'll find the free-roamer can outscore all other methods, but quite often it is best used as a means of searching out the pike before placing an anchored paternostered or legered bait in the swim.

The float-paternoster is a versatile and effective pike-taking tactic, but it is very misunderstood. These days, pike anglers seem to have embraced the sunken float-paternoster method almost to the exclusion of the once-popular surface-fished float paternoster rig, but I believe their catches suffer for it.

I first started working on the sunken paternoster idea more than 12 years ago in a bid to solve a problem—notably nuisance boat traffic—on a water I was fishing at the time. It proved to be very effective, fished in conjunction with the prototype Backbiter alarms Eddie Turner was experimenting with at that time, so together we developed the idea further ... eventually arriving at the rig in such common use today.

The problem is that today's pikers often use it as a convenience method; if they use a sunken float rig they don't have to bother to accurately plumb the depth first! I cannot imagine how any angler can fish with any confidence without knowing something of the underwater top-

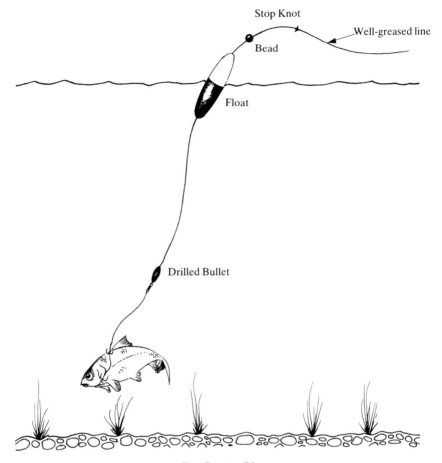

Free-Roamer Rig.

ography in his swim, but often these days this appears to be the norm.

Moreover, many pike anglers do not realise the big difference in presentation between livebaits fished on a sunken paternoster and those fished on a standard surface-float paternoster with an extended 'tail'. It was Barrie Rickards who first demonstrated to me how much extra water can be covered by a livebait fished on the latter method. The bait swimming on a sunken float rig is, of course, restricted to a very small area (which is useful in tight, snaggy swims or between weedbeds).

Although the paternoster fished with the float on the surface is a

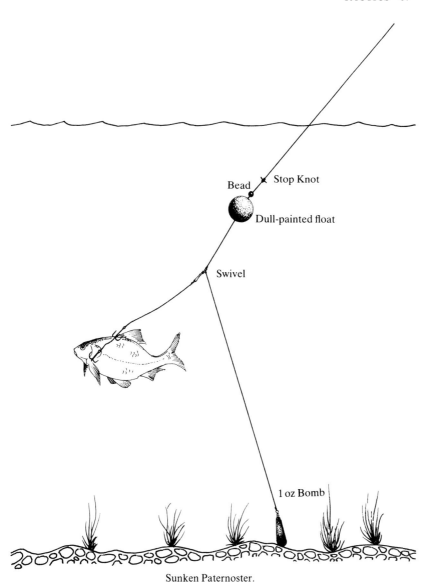

Bead   Stop Knot

Dull-painted float

Swivel

1 oz Bomb

Sunken Paternoster.

little more fiddly to get right, it will certainly pay dividends in terms
of pike tempted. On waters where pike have taken a bit of a hammering

Deadbaiting: Norfolk piker John Watson searches for pike on a big water.

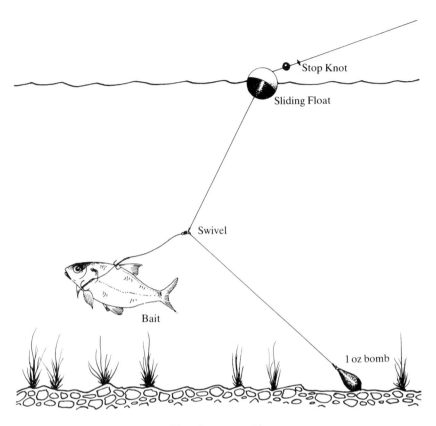

Float-Paternoster Rig.

on the sunken float-paternoster, they soon become wary of small fish swimming around unnaturally in tight circles. A bait fished on the surface float rig has a different action—and one which will often allay the suspicions of finicky pike.

In addition to the float-fishing methods so far described, it is also possible to fish livebaits on leger rigs. Provided the bait is of a modest size, you'll not suffer any problems from false runs. The legered livebait does score on some venues; I've had some success with it in the past on gravel pits, in particular, but I must admit it doesn't seem to be so effective as the various float rigs on most occasions.

Another factor the would-be livebait angler has to consider is the species of livebait he intends to use. Unfortunately, it is not possible in most areas to bring your own baits along to your chosen venue, due to strict regulations aimed at controlling the spread of fish diseases. The motive behind these restrictions is applaudable—nobody wants to see our waters infected with deadly viruses—but it is a shame allowance has not been made for anglers to bring certified disease-free rainbow trout baits along with them. Small trout make excellent baits and, as John Bailey so rightly said a couple of years ago, they are literally bred to die. Is it not better that we use such fish on our rigs rather than bait up with valuable stock fish that our fellow anglers would like to catch?

Trout do make excellent livebaits, provided the angler is alert to the possibility of an over-active bait causing tangles. Any bait that swims up and gets entangled around the reel line will lead to a bite-off if a pike takes and the mono comes into contact with its teeth. Rudd and dace are also a problem in this respect, as both tend to swim upwards, particularly during the warmer months.

Crucian carp, chub, small bream, roach and perch all make excellent livebaits, as do small samples of most of our coarse fish species.

Many anglers argue that livebaiting is the most natural presentation the pike angler can achieve, but that of course is simply untrue. A tethered livebait is a very unnatural form of presentation, since wild fish do not swim in the manner of a fish attached to a snap tackle. To my mind, the humble dead roach legered on the bottom is the closest we can come to presenting a bait in the way a pike would expect to find it.

And the roach lying on the bottom does indeed pick up the odd fish. I particularly like to fish one close in at the foot of the near shelf, because that is where a lot of match and pleasure anglers' keepnet casualties must most often end up.

Not that the pike always agree with my theories on perfect presentation, of course. I have to admit that I have caught a lot more pike on dead natural baits by fishing them off the bottom—namely in mid-water. You'd expect a pike to bolt for cover if it comes across a dead roach hovering suspiciously in mid-water, but the suspended deadbait is a neglected tactic that can sometimes prove devastating.

I caught my first pike on a suspended deadbait 20 years ago ... after I had run out of livebaits one day! And after that first success I picked up a few more over the years, usually in the same circumstances. I suppose I must have been more than a little slow on the uptake, because it wasn't until 1977 that I began to realise that the suspended deadbaits were very often producing many more pike than the livebaits. At that time I had obtained permission to fish a private stretch of the tiny River

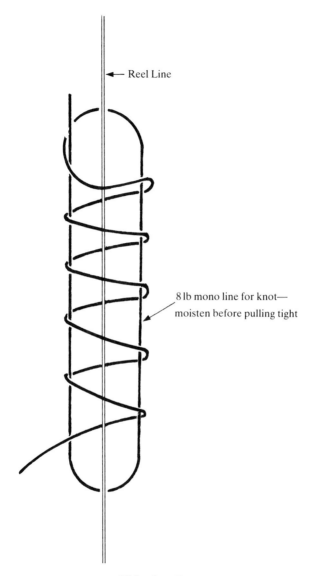

←— Reel Line

8 lb mono line for knot—
moisten before pulling tight

Sliding Stop Knot.

Babingley in west Norfolk where, for some unknown reason, the method produced twice as many pike as all other tactics put together.

It was a little wrinkle I never forgot—a method to keep up my sleeve and pull out whenever the going got tough. The chance came when a favourite Fen drain—a noted deadbait water—failed to go by the book one season. Some big catches were made on paternostered livebaits that autumn as the big pike in the water apparently abandoned their former taste for deadbaits legered hard on the bottom. Word quickly got out and several pikers in the area made some excellent bags on livebaits, including several 100 lb-plus catches and individual specimens to over 30 lb.

Those bonanza days were the norm until the winter weather set in, when suddenly blanks became more common. Static legered deadbaits were still near-useless, while it was obvious the pike were avoiding livebaits like the plague after the hammering they'd been taking. We were all tearing our hair out until, out of the blue, two big pike were taken by local youngsters in the traditional manner—i.e. a sprat fished three feet deep under a pike bung! This news caused some disgust among my colleagues at the time, but it sent alarm bells ringing in my head and it wasn't long before my suspended deadbaits were in action. Two useful double-figure pike fell to the method on my first effort and, while other anglers gave up the drain in disgust, I continued to catch several more good pike through that winter on the suspended deads.

Don't fall into the trap of ridiculing the beginner who manages to pull out a big pike on a suspended sprat. The angler may have been fortunate, but the pike didn't take it by chance; it accepted his bait because it wanted to feed on it at that time in preference to whatever else was around. The pike is quite at liberty to feed whenever it wishes on non-ultra-cult offerings!

To most anglers, of course, the standard deadbait method is a seafish legered on the bottom ... and very effective it is too. There are some waters where pike never tire of eating the usual half-mackerel or herring offerings, despite being recaptured several times on the same baits. I have to admit that in the depths of winter there's nothing I enjoy more than deadbaiting on a water where the pike population is known to have a taste for such baits. I love experimenting with rigs and trying out various exotic baits. It's a habit I've had ever since 1979, when I discovered for the first time just how good smelts could be as deadbaits (talk about slow learner: I caught my first pike on a legered smelt in 1970, but never followed it up!).

The learning process of the pike is not very fast, in my opinion,

Lure of the pike: Unhooking a 17-pounder that snaffled a Big S plug.

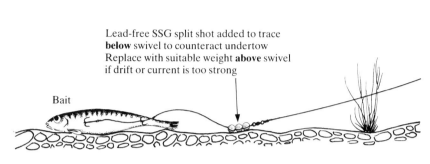

Lead-free SSG split shot added to trace
below swivel to counteract undertow
Replace with suitable weight **above** swivel
if drift or current is too strong

Bait

Leger Rig.

but nevertheless it is there. And that's why baits like smelt, sardines, snappers and eels have succeeded in tempting wary pike which have taken a pasting on the usual mackerel and herring baits. It is good fun trying out new baits and following in the footsteps of anglers like Neville Fickling and Dennis Smith, who have taken the technology a step further by dyeing their baits and adding artificial flavours, in the manner of the carp angler. Alternatively, on those waters where the ultra-cult boys are fishing nothing else but exotic baits, it's well worth a try casting out a humble whole herring ... because it could have been a long time since anybody tried anything that simple!

Whatever baits you decide to use, make sure you place them where you expect the pike to be. Contrary to popular opinion in some circles, pike aren't necessarily found at exactly the distance you can cast with a 13 ft rod, 3 oz bomb and a back wind! It may look macho to other anglers along the bank, but distance casting doesn't impress the pike. By all means hurl your baits out to the horizon if you have evidence that the pike are there, but on many waters you could find yourself casting over the heads of most of them.

As I said earlier, the foot of the near shelf is a favourite place to put a bait. Pike do patrol close to the bank, sometimes even when there is quite a lot of bankside activity. The near shelf and a little beyond it is a good area on most venues for catching most other species—and you can rest assured that the pike will never stray too far from their food supply. The margins are where keepnet casualties finish up on hard-fished waters, and they are also the place where pike anglers tend to discard their surplus baits at the end of a day's fishing. The food supply is there and so are the pike ... on more occasions than some anglers would believe.

The angler who fishes artificial lures for pike soon learns that his quarry can be found in the most unusual areas. It is quite common—and very frightening—to have a decent pike surge out from under your own bank to intercept your bait as you work it back to your casting position. In fact one of the biggest thrills in pike fishing must be that moment when you see a big pike take your lure in clear water. Pike are very adept at rendering themselves invisible to the casual observer, so the moment that three feet or so of pike materialises in front of your very eyes is bound to be a heart-stopping one.

I can certainly recommend summer lure fishing as a very enjoyable and effective way of locating pike; providing information that can prove useful later in the season when you're exploring those same waters with livebaits and deadbaits. Not that lure fishing is a surrogate form of pike fishing, of course; it is a very enjoyable method of fishing in its own right. I have to admit that I find it the most enjoyable way of catching them.

On most of the waters I have fished with lures, the pike are more widespread during the warmer months. But the hotspots and holding areas that produce the big pike catches in autumn and winter almost invariably prove good in the summer months too. Those spots which show plenty of activity to plugs and spoons during the June–September period are the places to head for with the livebaits and deadbaits from October onwards.

Not that lure fishing is a method only for the summer. It is certainly most effective during the warmer weather, but it also has its days throughout the winter. I've yet to take a 20 lb-plus pike on artificial baits, but my mid-winter catches to plugs include a 19 lb 1 oz beauty and several other doubles to 17 lb.

The biggest problem for the budding lure angler is the cost of the baits, for plugs, spoons and spinnerbaits can be very expensive. Take a look inside the tackle box of the lure enthusiast and you'll probably see a fortune invested in wood, metal and plastic baits. Some top American plugs can cost upwards of £10 in this country.

But it's not necessary to spend a fortune in order to catch pike on artificials. One of the best pike producers of all time, the Shakespeare Big S plug, only costs about £2.50 and it is easily obtained from most tackle shops. Daiwa, Rapala and Abu baits are also easy to get your hands on at a reasonable price, while some of value-for-money Canadian-

Bottom feeder: A float-legered herring accounted for this 23 lb Fenland pike.

made Kwikfish range, imported by the TG Lure Co, are also found in many of the better tackle shops. Spoons, of course, are very inexpensive ... and also quite easy to make for yourself.

Lures can be cast from the bank or trolled behind a moving boat. The latter tactic is a specialised method used for taking pike on larger waters, principally the big loughs of Ireland and the Scottish lochs. Few English waters lend themselves to trolling, since most are too small and, of those that are large enough, the majority are trout reservoirs where trolling with pike lures is in any case out of the question.

Since trolling has such a limited application in this country, I won't go into great detail on the method. Suffice it to say that the angler has to be proficient in boatcraft and must use a sonic echo-sounding device to enable him to follow a specific depth contour. The troller follows that specific line and uses a lure to suit the chosen depth. For example, by following the 12-foot contour, the angler will be able to safely troll plugs that are known to dive to about 10 feet or so. In practice, in clear water,

I prefer to fish lures that I know will work about four or five feet off the bottom, as feeding pike will launch themselves up off the bottom to take a well-worked bait . . . and many of the pike are already in midwater anyway. As I said earlier, pike most certainly do not spend all their time feeding on and around the bottom.

In trolling, an outboard motor is not essential—a good oarsman can maintain a reasonable trolling speed—but certainly desirable. I normally use a 4 horse-power Mariner outboard while boat fishing, and tickover on that engine generally provides the ideal trolling speed on most waters, on most days. Remember, however, that strong winds and currents have a great effect upon boat speed; trolling down the lake at engine tickover speed with a strong back wind will be considerably faster than the return trip up the lake into the teeth of the wind with the engine running at the same speed.

Of course, a boat is the ideal fishing platform for the pike angler on virtually any venue. It is possible to get to areas of any river or lake which are difficult or impossible to reach from the bank. And by moving in closer to fish and not having to resort to long-range tactics, the boat angler enjoys a considerable advantage in bait presentation.

On the Norfolk Broads, for example, boat fishing is imperative. Just a few very short stretches of Broadland's rivers are accessible to the bank angler; 99% of this area's shallow, fertile pike-holding grounds are only approachable by boat. My own best pike, a 27½ lb Broads beauty, was taken from a spot several hundred yards—and more than a few reedbeds!—away from the nearest point of dry land.

Boat fishing also lends itself to another of my favourite tactics—namely float-trolling. Again, this is a method that is often not permissible on many venues, but where it is allowed it is usually deadly. Like the trolling artificials man, the float-troller uses an echo-sounder to guide him along a specific depth contour, but instead of trailing a plug or spoon behind the boat, the float-troller inches along the contour with a float-fished livebait in tow.

Although I had a vague idea of the method as practised on the vast Dutch canal systems by continental anglers, it was the results of Steve Harper and friends on Norfolk's River Bure more than ten years ago that first grabbed my attention. By using a boat to steer a livebait close to the pikey margins of that busy Broadland river, Steve and his friends extracted some superb fish.

My best results to the method came a couple of years ago during four fantastic trips to Ardingly Reservoir in Sussex, during which my

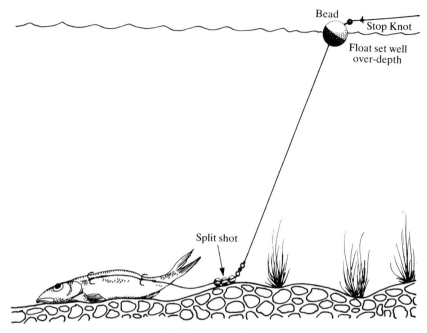

Bead
Stop Knot
Float set well
over-depth
Split shot

Float-Leger Rig.

friends and myself managed to land no less than four pike over 25 lb, all to float-trolled livebaits. It was truly incredible fishing on a water that, sadly, soon went into decline ... for reasons we will examine in the next chapter.

For now, suffice it to say that the float-trolled livebait, properly presented, was by far and away the most effective method at that time on Ardingly, a put-and-take trout reservoir with a relatively meagre stock of pike. The thoughtful pike angler could decide upon which areas seemed most capable of producing pike, then cover a lot of water—and several fish—by working a bait through them from the boat.

Word got out quite quickly that float-trolling was the method at Ardingly, but many anglers failed to capitalise on the knowledge by being too lazy. Electric trolling motors were available for hire at the venue and many used them to avoid the hard graft of rowing a dinghy around the reservoir all day long. However, the electric outboards, even at their lowest speed, were still too fast to effect perfect bait presentation on

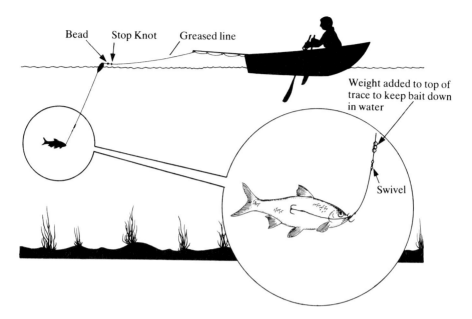

Float-Trolling.

most days during Ardingly's finest winter. To fish the float-trolled livebait efficiently, it is normally essential to trail it through the water very slowly.

What is the correct speed? Well, I fish my float-trolled livebaits in conjunction with a sliding float and if the line pulls through the float during the troll, I know I am rowing too fast. Amazingly, many of the anglers fishing Ardingly actually invented 'ingenious' ways of stopping their floats from slipping back up the line while they were trolling under electric power, without realising that they were missing out on optimum results by travelling too fast.

Although spring and summer pike will readily snatch a bait moving quite quickly through the water, English pike during the winter months appear to prefer to take a good look at the offering before committing themselves to strike.

By all means buy yourself an electric outboard. I use one myself—the excellent Shakespeare model—for exploring the smaller venues where my petrol outboard would be noisy and intrusive. The electric outboard is a quiet, pollution-free alternative, but it is still less effective than oars for the float-trolling enthusiast.

The proud owner of a new electric outboard should also realise that he has to meet the cost of a specialised battery in order to get a full day's fishing from his new purchase. A standard car battery is designed for maximum cranking and not a slow, steady drain on its charge. The electric outboard requires a very expensive boat or caravan battery for maximum efficiency.

But however you decide to tackle your chosen pike venue, from bank or boat, I'm sure you will have realised by now that this branch of the sport is open to all manner of approaches. The tactics I have described in this chapter are just a starting point in your quest for pike. No doubt in time you will evolve your own specialised variants of the tactics I have described in order to extract pike on your own patch. I hope you do, for the thinking, versatile angler with the innovative approach will always be the most successful.

Buccaneer Burton: Gord prepares to plunder a pikey-looking stretch of the River Shannon.

Tidal surge: The lower reaches of the River Nene near Wisbech, Cambridgeshire, produced this beautiful 15 lb pike to a paternostered livebait offered by local angler Steve Hicks.

Back-end beauty: This March-caught Fens pike was taken on an eel section bait.

Perfect hunter: A good pike lying in shallow water.

Jaws: The business end of a double-figure pike.

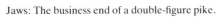

Prey's eye view: Of a predator.

Deadly: Lures from the Kwikfish stable.

Big S: Inexpensive plugs from Shakespeare.

Surface baits: Crazy Crawler, Heddon's Lucky 13 and Bass Oreno.

Conservation

I trust that by now I have given the reader a no-nonsense insight into the world of the modern pike angler and provided enough practical information to get you started and help you put a number of pike on the bank. But before you rush down to the waterside to get among 'em, you must first learn how to hook, land and handle your catch.

In the past, the majority of pike landed even by committed pike anglers were killed. Sometimes these fish were killed for the pot or a glass case, but more often they died in the mistaken belief that predator removal would 'improve' the fishery. Today, except in fairly isolated areas of the country, the situation has reversed and most pike are returned.

It is hard to argue against the logic of going to catch a pike with the intent of eating it; it is the epitome of the man-hunter instinct which is latent within all of us. However, killing pike for any reason is a luxury that we cannot afford these days when our fisheries are so crowded. Most pike in most fisheries are caught several times during their lives, so it doesn't take a genius to ascertain that the sport of most anglers would suffer if we all elected to kill the pike we caught.

I can quote numerous instances of big pike that have been returned to the water and then caught again at greater weights by other fortunate anglers. A prime example is the famous River Thurne former record pike, first caught by Neville Fickling at 41 lb-plus early in 1985. If Neville hadn't returned it safely to the water, it wouldn't have grown a further 1 lb and enabled Derek Amies to catch it and surpass the record a few months later.

On a smaller and more personal scale, my own first 20 lb-plus pike from a small Fenland drain was carefully returned to the water after I first caught it in February 1971. Ten months later, ironically, Neville Fickling caught it at the same weight from the very same spot! I'm pleased to say that even in our formative years as piking-mad schoolmates, Neville and I were conservationists.

Nev's best: Careful handling by Neville Fickling ensured that this 41 lb-plus pike survived to be caught again at a record weight by Derrick Amies.

Winding down: Eddie Turner leans into a good pike that picked up a bait at long range on a gravel pit.

And today, two decades on, the argument is even stronger. We live on an island where water space is hardly great enough to support the many people who want to take advantage of it. As anglers we all mutter disapproval in varying degrees at the other water-users and their demands, but windsurfers, water-skiers, yachtsmen and bird-watchers have much in common with anglers ... insofar as they all have a love for spending their leisure time by the waterside. It is up to us to ensure we all get along together as harmoniously as possible. And, likewise, even non-pikers should recognise the importance of the pike in our freshwater food chain.

Some matchmen and pleasure anglers, and even the late, great, Dick Walker, had little time for pike in the past. But in the Green 1990's it seems that environmentally-conscious anglers have come to realise that Mother Nature had it right all along; pike have their place in the general scheme of things. Who are we, as terrestrial mammals, to interfere in the delicate balance of life in the hidden depths of our fisheries? It is no coincidence that the very best general coarse fisheries in this land also happen to be very prolific pike waters!

Now, with that lot off my chest, let's get down to the bankside and set about catching some pike. Provided you are using one of the modes of bite indication I outlined earlier, you will have no problems in detecting a run and knowing when a pike has grabbed hold of your bait. In most cases the pike will indeed 'run' off with your offering, taking several yards of line with it, although there are quite a few venues where takes are more finicky and the pike will sometimes swallow the bait on the spot.

Either way, the last thing you want is a deeply-hooked pike, so don't be afraid of striking as soon as you know your bait has been taken. Despite the advice contained within some old textbooks, it is not necessary to wait until the pike has turned the bait or made off on its second run before you strike the hooks home.

As soon as you know a pike is on the business end of your line, close the bale arm of your reel and wind down to the fish until you can feel it on the end. At this stage an actual strike in the accepted sense is not necessary—it is better to carry on winding and positively pull the hooks home with a low and steady sweep of the rod, keeping a very tight line to the pike all the time.

It is unlikely that the angler could actually strike the hooks home himself once a pike had its powerful jaws clamped around a bait. It is more a case of waiting for the pike to feel the resistance on the line caused by the angler, panicking and shaking its head, driving the hooks home for you as it releases its vice-like grip on the bait.

Compared to other forms of angling, the striking of a pike run does appear unconventional. But, believe me, the angler who adopts any other approach will be disappointed in terms of missed runs and pike which manage to shed the hooks in the early stages of the fight.

Probably because of the apparent difficulty of hooking pike with a short, sharp strike, many beginners leave their runs far too long, in the hope that they can hook their pike in the fleshy throat tissue instead of chancing a hookhold in amongst the teeth and bony sections of the pike's mouth. But to deliberately set out to hook pike in the throat is both unsporting and illegal. Although it is highly unlikely that the angler would ever actually be prosecuted for gorge-baiting, he will have to live with the knowledge that he has caused certain harm to his catch and that it may well die through his selfish actions. Pike are quite hardy creatures and many do live after the careful removal of deeply-seated hooks,

Fighting fury: The writer's rod takes on an alarming curve as he stops a scrapping
Scottish pike from seeking sanctuary around the boat's anchor rope.

Enmeshed: A good drains pike in the net for Steve Hicks.

Coming in: Barrie Rickards about to net a small pike.

but the angler who deliberately sets out to hook his quarry deeply is a fool and has no right to be in charge of a pike rod.

Sadly, even a minority of our so-called 'serious' pike anglers frequently leave runs far too long and hook their catch deeply. Some believe that their pike come to no harm if they use barbless hooks, but the fact is that barbless hooks usually penetrate more deeply than their barbed counterparts and, if seated well down the throat of a pike, can actually damage internal organs and cause the pike a slow, lingering death.

All successful pike anglers sometimes hook their catches too deeply; there are always the occasional individual fish that swallow baits rapidly to the throat before the angler has a chance to strike. Even in lure fishing, the pike angler will frequently come across avidly-feeding fish that swallow the bait to the back of the throat before a strike can be made. But all this is no excuse for deliberately hooking them deeply.

Later in this chapter we'll discuss how best to unhook the pike which have swallowed hooks further than the angler intended, but in the meantime let me assure the reader that a very quick strike is all you need to drive the hooks home securely, provided you follow the rules of striking that I outlined earlier.

Quite frequently I have in the past fished swims where instant striking of pike runs was imperative due to the nature of the underwater geography. For example, during the autumn of 1983 Eddie Turner and I spent a lot of time on a large Bedfordshire clay pit which was a veritable jungle of sunken trees and bushes. And we soon discovered that the very best spots for finding big pike on this venue was right in amongst the densest snags.

Obviously legered baits were out of the question and the only way of presenting a bait to the pike in their lairs was to set up a float paternoster, using a six-foot leger link with a 'rotten bottom' of weak line which would break free if snagged.

Once cast out, the line from the rig was wound tight back to the rod and the line clipped into an ET Backbiter drop-off alarm. As soon as a run was registered it was necessary to literally leap into action— closing the bail arm, winding tight and fast and hauling the pike to the net before it could reach the sanctuary of the snags. We used 15 lb Sylcast and 3 lb test curve rods to accomplish this heavy-handed approach.

Despite this instant striking, one pike still managed to swallow a bait deeply. Yet the rest were all lightly hooked in the corner of the jaw and none managed to shake out the hooks on the way to the net.

By adopting the striking procedure I have described, very few of

Gently does it: The writer unhooks a herring-caught pike without removing it from
the water—thus avoiding the possibility of it damaging itself by thrashing around
in the boat.

Open wide: Graham Billing unhooks a big reservoir pike that wolfed down a deadbait.

your pike will be hooked deeply, although one or two greedy individuals will inevitably wolf down baits before you can physically get to the rod and strike. To unhook these, forget about old-fashioned gags and long-nosed pliers. All you need is a sturdy pair of artery forceps—available from any tackle dealer.

If the hooks are deep, embedded in the gill rakers or the soft tissue at the back of the throat, gently lay your capture on its back on a suitable surface—like the soft ET Unhooking Mat I mentioned earlier. Sit astride the pike, holding it firmly in position, and place the fingers of your left hand under the gill flaps on its lower jaw. You will find that the pike's mouth will open—and stay open—quite easily.

Gently pull the trace and any deep-seated hooks will come into sight. These can be reached by putting the business end of the (closed) forceps through the opening at the rear of the gill cover and carefully releasing the hooks. Any hooks out of sight in the soft throat tissue are best removed by inverting them with the forceps. Pull the trace firmly until the shank of the hook appears in view, then grip it with the forceps and turn it

Steadying influence: By sitting with his knees gently astride a double-figure pike,
Steve Hicks can get down to unhooking it safely.

upside-down. Gentle manoeuvring should clear the flesh from the points of the treble.

If the hooks are completely out of sight and gentle pulling on the trace does not bring them into view, it is probably best to cut the trace as close to the hooks as possible and hope that the pike's digestive juices quickly corrodes the hooks. Past evidence suggests that this is quite often the case, but sadly many pike left with hooks down their throats are later found dead in the margins. A few careless anglers can soon ruin a pike fishery by hooking their catches too deeply.

Likewise, strike and play your pike carefully, as a snap-off can be even more dangerous. A treble hook firmly seated in the 'scissors' of a pike's jaw will prevent it from opening its mouth, which in turn will stop it from feeding or even breathing properly. The lure angler should be particularly vigilant in this respect, as a pike with a large plug wedged firmly in the corner of its mouth stands little chance of survival.

The best way for the novice to learn how to safely handle and unhook his pike is to go along to a teach-in organised by the Pike Anglers' Club of Great Britain. This national organisation has many local branches, each comprising several experienced pike anglers who are only too willing to demonstrate the practical methods of dealing with the pike on the bank.

It shouldn't prove too difficult for even an inexperienced angler to get a big pike safely to the bank for unhooking. Pike in big, clear waters do fight quite hard, and have quite a lot of stamina in the summer months, but the correct rod should do most of the work for you, absorbing the fighting lunges of a hooked pike. Nylon monofilament line also has a lot of stretch and the likelihood of a really scrappy pike breaking free on sound tackle only becomes a possibility on a short line, close to the net. Be very careful when a good pike is close to the bank and apparently played out, as it will usually find a whole new lease of life when confronted with the prospect of being hauled into a landing net!

When playing a pike on a fixed-spool reel I prefer to backwind rather than rely upon the clutch, but that is a matter of personal choice. Either way, make sure you are able to give line if the pike decides to make a sudden late surge.

Netting the pike is straightforward, provided you remember the golden rule that applies when netting all fish: sink the net beforehand. Don't lift it until the pike's bulk is well over the rim of the frame. Complications can arise when one set of hooks from the snap tackle is outside the pike's mouth; many a big pike has escaped at the last moment because

Deep hooks: Can be removed safely by inserting the forceps through the pike's gill flap.

the hooks have got tangled in the mesh before the pike was actually over the frame.

If there are hooks flying around outside the pike's mouth, I prefer to land the pike by hand instead, although I realise this latter procedure can be tricky at first for the beginner or the younger angler with a smaller handspan. Pike up to 10 lb or so, however, are quite easy to land in this way, provided they are played out. Grip the subdued specimen immediately behind its head and lift smoothly and quickly onto the bank. Bigger pike should be grasped by inserting the forefinger and second finger of the right hand into the gill flap before lifting the pike ashore. It is quite easy with a little practice.

The less handling your pike receives, the sooner it will recover from the experience of being hooked and landed. If you do not want to weigh and photograph modest specimens, it is advisable to unhook them in the water, touching them as little as possible. Pike, like all fish, are covered in a protective slime to ward off fungus and other water-borne diseases. This slime is soon damaged once a pike is out of the water.

Once the pike is unhooked, it is time for the angler to weigh his catch—provided it is large enough to warrant the scales, of course. Some novice pike anglers come unstuck at this stage, discovering that their scales just aren't big enough to weigh a very big fish. These days I carry a Salter 44 lb brass spring balance for this job rather than a set of 32 lb Avon dial scales. The latter are excellent scales, but there is the outside chance that you might latch into a pike of more than 32 lb . . .

Pike can be weighed by placing the hook of the balance under their chins, but this can be a very dicey practice even in experienced hands. What was a very docile pike will often find a sudden new lease of life once hoisted off the ground, and if it falls heavily onto the bank it could end up badly damaged. It is better instead to invest in a good weigh sling to avoid any danger of injuring a heavy fish.

Various types of weigh sling are available, but there is no doubt that the 'shopping bag' type is the safest for the pike and easier to use. ET Products and The Tackle Shop, Gainsborough, both market excellent versions. Incidentally, don't forget to wet the sling before placing any fish in it, as a dry nylon sling will remove much of the pike's slime. And remember to either zero your scales with the sling or deduct the weight afterwards, or you will enhance the true weight of your catches by several ounces!

Unless I am retaining a big pike while preparing the photographic equipment for a trophy shot, I always return my fish straight back to

Sack race: Dave slides a big pike out of the sack for a quick photo session.

Photo session: John Watson holds a good River Bure pike for the camera.

the water after weighing. There is no harm in keeping a fish in a Pike Tube or big, well-designed carp sack for a few minutes, but pike should never be retained in keepnets and at no stage should more than one specimen be placed in a sack. Anchor the retaining cord securely to a fixed bankside object and make sure you place the sack or tube in oxygenated water, as deep as possible. If in doubt, don't retain it.

As far as photography goes, it is up to the angler how much he wants to invest in photographic equipment to record his catches, but there is no doubt that a nice collection of angling photographs is a pleasure to look back on from time to time. I personally use 35 mm SLR equipment, but the modern auto-focus, auto-exposure compact cameras costing as little as £60 will certainly produce very pleasing results. A fuss-free camera will also allow the angler to get trophy photographs taken as quickly as possible; a pike kept out of the water for more than a couple of minutes in hot or windy weather will suffer as its slime dries up very quickly in those conditions.

The angler who fishes alone, far from the crowds, should make sure

Going back: Gently returning a 20 lb-plus pike to the water.

he takes a camera with a self-timer facility and an adaptor that allows him to fix it to a bankstick.

Finally, the pike should be returned to the water gently. Never drop your fish into the margins, but instead lower them slowly and slide them back. Some pike, particularly those which have scrapped hard, may be exhausted and should be held firmly but gently upright in the water until they are strong enough to swim away comfortably.

And that, at the end of the day, is perhaps the most important thing you must learn. The very future of pike fishing depends upon thoughtful, modern anglers practising not only the most effective tactics to maximum advantage but employing them in such a way that their quarry comes to minimum harm. Many top pike fisheries have literally been ruined by the careless actions of anglers.

Big pike are less numerous on some waters than many anglers believe.

Repeat captures of individual fish build up a false picture of pike stocks to the inexperienced angler. Even on superb waters like Ardingly Reservoir, where no pike were deliberately killed, heavy angling pressure over a period of little more than a year saw pike sport go into decline. It is likely that in this water a reduced intake of stocked trout exacerbated the situation, but either way the incredible pike sport on that venue, which I described in the previous chapter, soon came to an end.

Top angler Jim Gibbinson once said that big pike thrive on neglect. How right he was. I know of no pike fisheries which have ever improved once subject to heavy angling pressure.

It should by now be plain to the reader that consistent success with specimen pike can be achieved with the application of a little effort and a lot of thought. The competent angler with the right bait in the right place at the right time should soon be catching pike of 10 lb or more, with the occasional 20-pounder thrown in for good measure. That's what I would describe as enjoyable, bread-and-butter pike fishing.

But it must also be stressed that venues like Ardingly Reservoir in its heyday, where large numbers of 25 lb-plus pike were taken during a short period of time, are exceptional. When Ardingly first opened its gates to pike anglers it was an unexploited resource; a rich yet established put-and-take trout reservoir with additional ample stocks of roach, bream and hybrids. Its pike had waxed fat, unmolested by man. Moreover, the fact that the then fishery manager, Colin Simpson, decided to allow any-method pike fishing, made those pike very accessible to the anglers keen to pit their wits against them.

The anglers who enjoyed most success with the big pike at Ardingly were those who got in there early. It is still a good fishery today, but it does not compare with the standard of sport enjoyed there in 1986 and 1987.

The history of pike fishing is liberally dotted with venues like Ardingly; waters which, with their dazzling successes in their day, put all other places into the shade. With few exceptions, most faded into obscurity after a few years of glory. Other factors often played a part in the decline of these waters, but the biggest significant setback they each endured was pressure of angling from pikers.

The smaller and more accessible the fishery, the shorter its lifespan as a top pike water will be. The Fen drains suffer in particular from intense angling pressure, for there is no hiding place for the pike on most of these open, artificial waterways of East Anglia. The larger Irish loughs and wildernesses like Norfolk's upper Thurne system can take

Bucket mouth: An Irish pike that wished it had kept its mouth shut.

Winter wonder: A beautifully-marked big pike that accepted a half-mackerel bait during the grip of a freeze-up.

more pressure, however, for there are plenty of areas of sanctuary where the pike can escape the angler.

And it is the intense pressure on this country's quality pike fishing that in turn has led to the less-than-exemplary behaviour of some specimen hunters. All too often the specialist pike angler faces fierce competition from fellow anglers on the better pike waters, which in turn to leads to friction, jealousy and even physical violence. Undesirable bankside behaviour gives not just pike fishing a bad name, but provides ammunition for those who would prefer angling to be outlawed.

Non-angling members of the public don't notice unobtrusive anglers as they walk their dogs by the waterside or take their families on boating holidays. But they *do* remember the foul-mouthed yobs and the litter louts; it is the offensive minority of anglers that get noticed and they that put the whole future of angling in jeopardy. Play your part in setting an example on the bankside, or you could arrive for a pike session one day and find angling has been banned on your favourite water.

Perhaps we do take it all too seriously sometimes. After all, catching plenty of big, beautiful pike should actually be enjoyed, you know! We are guilty of getting too obsessive about our fishing from time to time; I know that in the past I have suffered the frustrations of finding a water difficult to crack and made other people's lives unbearable as a result. It's not a bad idea sometimes to take a step backwards and try to take an objective look at what you are doing. Not only will this help you put your situation into perspective, it may well show where you are going wrong.

It's not the end of the world if you suffer a blank or two; you're not a failure because you've yet to 'crack' the 20 lb barrier. Luck does play a part in pike fishing, but you can help make your own luck by fishing in the right frame of mind. The positive angler who is enjoying his fishing is more likely to hit a purple patch than the paranoid piker who is letting his frustrations prevent him from thinking straight.

Pike angling is not an endurance test. If things are really going badly, it's often a good idea to take a couple of weekends off and fish for another species, get drunk, dig the garden or whatever. You'll end up refreshed and raring to get back among the pike.

A blinkered attitude does not help at all. I sometimes wonder whether the increasing specialisation within angling is bad for the sport, for I believe it breeds intolerance and bigotry. To understand other branches of angling, it helps to have actually given them a try at some time. These days, many young anglers actually enter the sport as out-and-out pike

An old friend: This pike from Norfolk's Middle Level drain put in two appearances to the author's rod in the space of ten months, weighting 25 lb 14 oz at its heaviest and proving how vulnerable Fenland pike are to repeat captures.

Budding piker: A young angler who can expect some first-class sport before the century is out if pike fishing is allowed on the big trout reservoirs.

anglers, carp specialists or budding matchmen. And the sad thing is that many of them quit angling completely after enduring a frustrating season of realising that there are no short cuts to beat watercraft and experience.

The best pike anglers I have ever met are also adept at other aspects of the sport. John Watson and John Sidley are both brilliant eel anglers; Neville Fickling is the country's top zander man. Even Eddie Turner used to impress the kids on the banks of the River Lea by whipping out bleak on the pole! Give any of those anglers a swim and a rod and they'll be fishing . . . and catching.

So what of the future? Where does pike fishing fit in on the threshold of a new decade, with the 21st century just around the corner?

I believe piking will continue to be one of angling's major growth areas for some years to come and I'm also convinced that new thinking in fisheries management, as well as pure economics, will provide the pike angler with a host of exciting new opportunities. Keen pike anglers have proved time and time again that they are prepared to part with considerable sums of hard cash in pursuit of exceptional pike and, with the privatisation of the water authorities, enterpreneurial fisheries managers will be only to pleased to welcome the pikers on the big water supply reservoirs.

Scientific facts demonstrate that culling pike on trout reservoirs is actually a waste of time as well as prohibitively expensive. Waters like Grafham and Rutland will one day become havens for big pike and we, the pike anglers, will be allowed to fish for them in the manner we choose. We'll rub shoulders with the trout anglers and we'll enjoy each others' company, because we'll each know that our best interests are served by mixed trout and pike fisheries.

The pike angler knows that pike have the pleasing habit of packing on the pounds in the big reservoirs which receive a supplement in the shape of thousands of farm-reared trout. And the trout angler will soon recognise that the income generated by allowing pike anglers to pay for the privilege of fishing these waters will in turn pay for even more quality brown and rainbow trout.

The angling world took a bit of a shock when Llandegfedd Reservoir in South Wales produced its first crop of big pike to rod and line late in 1988, but Gareth Edwards' 45-pounder early in 1990 was a vindication for those who, like myself, put their necks on the block back in 1986 by insisting that it would be the best pike fishery in Europe, if only it was opened up to pike anglers. The success of the limited piking trials at Llandegfedd have demonstrated for all time that pike and trout do

John Sidley: A very successful pike angler who is also one of the country's top
eel specialists.

Thinking angler: John Watson takes a break from piking ... but is he dreaming
of a 30 lb pike swimming in that pint of Guinness?

New technology: Pike anglers in the future will learn the full potential of the science of lure fishing.

mix—and pave the way to a new era of incredible sport for us all.

Opening up the great trout reservoirs to the pike men will also provide breathing space on our present pike fisheries, which are already under such intense pressure. Happily, angling is governed by the same economic laws of supply and demand as the rest of life in the western world and the hordes of pikers hungry for big pike are going to be catered for now that businessmen have replaced the water authority bureaucrats who once ruled our big reservoirs from their ivory towers.

Unfortunately, there is a very real chance that the pike angler of the future will be limited as to *how* he elects to catch his pike. Too many ineffectual self-styled angling politicians have already offered livebaiting as a sacrifice on the altar dedicated to appeasing the anti-angling factions of our society. Many misguided angling associations and bodies have already outlawed livebaiting for pike, and plenty more are sure to follow suit as the century draws to a close. There is, in my opinion, also a strong possibility that a future government will get embroiled in the whole question of country sports. I pray that we can boast an effective new generation of leaders before angling practices come under parliamentary scrutiny.

There is, therefore, no time like the present for British pike anglers to catch up with the rest of the northern hemisphere and learn how to make the most of the current techniques and technology in the world of artificial lures. Even committed lure enthusiasts like myself are only scratching the surface of the potential of using and working these baits to their full advantage.

It is especially important to recognise that artificial lures are very effective indeed on the very waters I have been describing in the preceding paragraphs; the plug, spoon and spinnerbait have more than proved their worth on the big reservoirs for those prepared to give them more than a half-hearted cast and retrieve. Lure fishing for pike is destined to become very big indeed in the coming years.

In conclusion, I urge you to get out there on the bankside and make the most of the fun that pike fishing can provide. Fish thoughtfully and conscientiously and remember that every time you catch a big pike you literally have the future of our sport in your hands.